My Travel Diary: 1936

BETWEEN TWO WORLDS

PAUL TILLICH

Edited and with an Introduction
by Jerald C. Brauer
Translation by Maria Pelikan
Drawings by Alfonso Ossorio

HARPER & ROW, PUBLISHERS
New York, Evanston, and London

Dedicated to Erdmuthe and Hannah

FIRST EDITION

LIBRARY OF CONGRESS CATALOG CARD NUMBER: 72-85047

Contents

Acknowledgment 7

Introduction 9

The Diary 27–184

Notes to Introduction 185

Glossary of Names 186

Acknowledgment

When Hannah Tillich first proposed the publication of her late husband's 1936 diary, several of us responded with enthusiasm, others had doubts. We believe that the public's reception of the diary will validate her decision. The editor is grateful for that decision and states his special appreciation to her for help at many points in the preparation of the manuscript. Years of friendship lay behind our discussions and our mutually supportive decision to move ahead with publication.

The editor wishes to thank Maria Pelikan for her translation of a difficult manuscript. In her case this was not simply the work of a professional but of a friend of the Tillichs. Hannah Tillich turned to another friend and a famous artist, Alfonso Ossorio, to provide interpretive drawings which enhance an understanding of the diary. This is most appropriate for Tillich's diary which is laced with references to art and artists. We are in Ossorio's debt for his creative interpretation of the diary's spirit.

Many people were consulted in an effort to establish certain facts and to identify names that appear in the diary. Particular thanks are due to Tillich's family in Berlin, where in the comfort of their homes I gained much information and insight. His sister and brother-in-law, Elisabeth and Pastor Erhardt Seeberger, and their family, Dr. Hans Jürgen Seeberger, Heide Schütz, and Waldtraub Le Fevre, provided

7

invaluable help. Hannah Tillich's sister, M. L. Werner of Berlin, spent hours with me in discussion. I am deeply grateful to all of these friends for their assistance and advice.

In addition, a number of Tillich's close friends worked personally with me in an effort to verify names and events. Professors Adolf Loewe, Walter Braune, and Wilhelm Pauck were most helpful. In London, Mrs. Lilly Pincus was more than generous with her time and hospitality and also obtained help from Mrs. Claire Loewenfeld. To all these people I wish to express my thanks. Finally, I wish to state my gratitude to my secretary Miss Alma Obrikat and to Miss Marilyn Karieba who typed the manuscript through several editions. Kent Druyvesteyn provided considerable help in reading proofs.

J. C. B.

Introduction
by Jerald C. Brauer

The year Paul Tillich made his first trip back to Europe, after his enforced emigration of 1933, was a time of escalating crisis and growing uncertainty. Just one month prior to Tillich's sailing in April, 1936, Hitler had denounced the Locarno Pact and had remilitarized the Rhineland. In July the Spanish Civil War broke out and provided an occasion for Hitler and Mussolini to cooperate in joint plans. Soon most major European powers were involved one way or another in the Spanish struggle. Meanwhile, the non-Fascist and non-Communist governments stood confused and ineffective before the determination and maneuvering of Hitler.

This was the context in which plans were laid for the churches' ecumenical Oxford and Edinburgh meeetings on faith and order as well as life and work. The central theme of the life and work conference in Oxford, 1937, was the interrelationships between church, community, and state. Theologians and churchmen, in search for Christian unity across national and denominational boundaries, saw and experienced the expanding conflict between Christianity and the growing secular and even pagan forces of the 1930s. The conflict was seen to be between expanding forms of state totalitarianism which divinized themselves in monopolizing all goals of life and the Christian interpretation of human nature and destiny.

9

In preparation for the Oxford conference a number of study groups were established throughout the world. Issues were explored, studies were undertaken, discussions were held, and publications were developed. Over a three-year period nine subjects were studied as background preparation. In the summer of 1936 one of these groups was to meet at Oxford to hear each other's paper, to discuss and to criticize prior to publication of the papers, and to continue exploration of the central problems on the agenda for the 1937 conference. Paul Tillich was invited to deliver one of the papers and to participate in the discussion on *The Kingdom of God and History*.

On this trip, lasting from April to September, 1936, Tillich kept a diary in which he recounted his daily experiences and personal reactions. As are most diaries, this is a highly personal document. He intended it to be read by his wife, for whom it was written, and his family, and it is clear he is not writing with any other audience in mind. It does not exhibit a high degree of consciousness of a public, nor does the diary indicate a concern for style or effect. This is a simple account of human experiences recorded in an almost spontaneous fashion.

What then is the value of the diary? Anybody who turns to it in search of new theological insights or for a fuller theological elaboration of Tillich's concepts will not find them. The diary adds nothing new to the corpus of his theological writings. That is not its value. The diary does provide many comments by Tillich on the world situation and on the pressing political problems of the mid-1930s, but these reveal nothing new concerning his interpretation of, or a stand on, such issues.

The value of the diary lies in the way it reveals the man as theologian. Paul Tillich was an unusual theologian in the way he theologized. Not only did he exhibit a highly creative, subtle, and profound theological analysis of life, he also went about his theologizing in a most extraordinary manner. It is not enough to say his theology was existential, though it undoubtedly was. Tillich's theology was a piece with his life and grew out of it. That was one point of his overwhelming appeal to modern men. He agonized over his tensions and problems as a modern man, thus he caught the imagination of modern men. He stood in the middle of the modern predicament and shared its frustrations, fears, and creativity. Tillich's theology was not an abstract creation forged out of the interplay of logic and concepts. It found its point of departure in his own existence—his own being. To read his diary is to understand better how he theologized.

No words can better describe Tillich the man and his theology than those words he applied to himself—"on the boundary."[1] His 1936 diary, the day-to-day account of his activities and reactions, clearly demonstrates how accurately he understood himself as a man who lived on the boundary and theologized out of that situation. The 1936 trip was his first return to Europe after his escape from Hitler, and he already saw himself as living between two worlds. He fully owned America as his new home, but a part of him remained in Europe, particularly Germany. One is astonished at the rapidity with which he identified himself with his new land. It is this which enabled him to live between two worlds.

Late in his life he had written, "Emigration at the age of forty-seven means that one belongs to two worlds: to the Old as well as to the New into which one has been fully received."[2] One is not surprised that emigration at such a late age meant that he remained very much a European. The diary illustrates this. He comments on his arrival in England, "with real European forests," and its difference "from the American landscape that has been ravaged by technology, and . . . from the forbidding wilderness to be found in many nonindustrial regions of America."[3] Already he was living between the two worlds, a part of each. Even in the debates over the upcoming Oxford conference, he found himself "standing on the boundary" between the two major points of view, "the Lutheran-German and the Anglo-Saxon."[4]

Equally divided was his deep feeling about Germany. As he was at the Edinburgh docks, he wrote in his diary that he had "two glimpses of the open North Sea—the native ocean of my heart. Over there, a little off to one side, to the southwest, lies Germany! Kampen!"[5] That was the spot where he spent so many memorable hours of summer vacation. Kampen was forever a part of him. The fact that he used an exclamation point after Germany should not be overlooked. Later, in May, as he traveled through Holland, he stopped "for lunch atop a mountain from where we can see all the way to Germany. I see it without any feeling of homesickness. Dead, destroyed; barbed wire and Gestapo."[6] When he visited Riehen, a tip of Basel surrounded by Germany on three sides, he said it gave him an "uncanny feeling, like being pushed into a sack."[7] However much he detested the Nazis, this could not destroy his love for his people and for his land. In Luxembourg he remarked how "the landscape is very German and close to my heart."[8]

The diary reveals that within three short years he came to identify with America in a remarkable way. It was his home, Americans were his people, and its landscape with its beauty and man-made ugliness were understood. He truly lived in that world. Yet he continued to live in Europe as well. He lived between the two worlds, and it took his first return to Europe to demonstrate that to him. This gave substance to the more profound elements in his experience of living on the boundary in all aspects of his life. For Tillich there was always both an outer and an inner emigration.[9] To part from ways of thinking, of believing, from traditions, from political commitments—all these represented inner emigration. Thus his experience of living between two worlds was a profound spiritual reality which marked every facet of his life.

The person who lives on the boundary is constantly risking oneself. One can easily lose himself in the risk of the boundary, but the essence of life is the risk of losing one's being in order to find it. Perhaps that is one aspect of Tillich's giving so much of himself to people. The most remarkable thing about the diary is the flood of people that pour over the pages. It seems impossible that one man could have known so many people—an astounding variety of people—professors, artists, musicians, politicians, students, businessmen, the great and the humble. He knew them and was concerned about them. To know a person does not mean to be acquainted with him. To know a person is to encounter him as someone with hopes, fears, convictions, dreams, pettiness, and generosity. Tillich's knowledge of people, of his friends, was of this quality. The diary reflects this with great clarity.

Perhaps one reason Tillich sought out so many people of widely varying types was precisely because he was risking his own being—living on the boundary between the center of his own strong personality and the diffusion of participating in genuine friendship with so many people. It would have been so much simpler and safer to confine himself to a manageable circle of friends, especially of a certain type. To have done so, however, would have meant the failure to go out of the center of self truly to encounter others. He appears to have constantly stretched himself in a dozen directions, as if he were testing himself. He certainly could have lost himself, his own center, in this vast diffusion of personal encounters. But that is the way he found himself—in the risk and in the constant giving of self.

This was a very important way for Tillich to remain in contact with the concrete, to participate in reality through countless deep personal relationships with people. In many places he recounted his struggle to live between theory and practice, and this is not to be lightly dismissed. He could have been as most philosophers and theologians, buried in the abstract both in thought and in practice—at no point participating deeply, existentially, in life itself. He had a genius for highly theoretical abstract thought that easily could have lost contact with men in history as they faced personal decisions, and experienced suffering, joy, alienation, and healing. However, he never permitted his unusual gift for abstract thought to cut him off from the human and the historical.

The diary shows a man who moved between disciplined thinking through lonely reflection in preparation for lectures or books and the give-and-take of friendship and discussion. He could write so perceptively about courage, suffering, or estrangement because he experienced it himself; not in solitary isolation, but in his deeply personal relationships with hundreds of human beings of such widely diverse types and professions. The diary enables one to understand better the remarkable insights into the human situation, both personal and social, developed by Paul Tillich the theologian and philosopher. This is due as much, perhaps even more, to his unusual involvement with people, individual specific people, as it is to his extraordinary theoretical gifts.

Tillich's breadth of concern and interest was exhibited in many directions. Again, one wonders how he managed to maintain a wholeness and coherence both in his life and in his work. Yet coherence is precisely what marked Paul Tillich, although it was not the coherence of a neat, ordered, logical consistency. It was an integrity that emerged from a man living in tension with manifold creative dimensions of experience in which he participated fully.

This wide participation did not destroy or undercut his central concern as theologian, it was only in that way he became the kind of theologian he was. His interest in politics, economics, art, literature, philosophy, theology, and people was both a consequence of, and formative for, his essential theological point of view. There was no realm of culture or society off limits for the theologian. It was at the depth, the very ground, of these forms that the infinite was encountered.

To confine himself only to biblical language or simply to

the history of the church's doctrine or dogma was impossible for Paul Tillich. To be sure, one ignored or temporized with these at the risk of destruction as a theologian, but their importance lay in the fact that they were the particular and unique forms in which the experience and the reality of the sacred grasped the Christian community. As a believing and participating member of that community such experience was primordial for Tillich, but it was not confining or restrictive.[10] It drove him to risk its reality and truth in as many facets of life as possible and later in encounters with other religions.[11]

The diary documents this wide-ranging interest and participation. He was, of course, deeply concerned and knowledgeable about the German situation. Everywhere he went he lectured about it, discussed it, and saw it in relation to the vast forces that reflected the movement of world history. In England he could not understand the reluctance of the Conservative government to face the reality of Nazism's threat. In most nations, only a few were sensitive to the *kairotic* moment in history. Tillich saw this question as one not primarily political in character, but multiform. It had to be seen in relation to the total human situation—the revolt against the bourgeois spirit which marked modern man. So he discussed economics, aesthetics, philosophy, education, science, literature, and sociology as well as politics in his lectures and with his friends.

It was his holistic concern for the historic moment that led him to propose his plan for an order or a group of leading Christian and concerned intellectuals to consider systematically the major political decisions confronting mankind. The diary makes a number of references to that idea, and he proposed it to Joseph Oldham. It would bring together men in positions of power and leading theoreticians so that between them they could concentrate combined resources on the analysis of major issues that confronted mankind. Thus, those in positions of power would be able to make more creative and constructive decisions in relation to the crises of history. Tillich envisioned this as a brotherhood of dedicated men working together in a common cause. Nothing seems to have come from the idea, though Oldham later developed an English group, the Christian Frontier Society, that was somewhat similar in structure and purpose.

The diary also reveals the integrity between Tillich's theology and his life with regard to nature. Anyone who reads his theology, quickly discovers that here is a modern Protestant theologian who has a conception of nature radically different from his contemporary Protestant theologians. It was once remarked that Calvin lived in the midst of the beauties of the Swiss Alps but never mentioned them. Perhaps that is not so important as, though it is related to, the way that nature is treated in Reformed theology particularly, and in Protestantism generally. Tillich saw a difference between classical Lutheran and Reformed dogmatics on this point as reflected in their respective doctrines of Christ. In the Reformed tradition the finite was radically separated from the infinite and incapable of bearing it. Lutheran Christology affirmed the interpretation of the human and the divine qualities in the Christ, though they remained qualitatively different.[12]

Tillich's religious tradition reinforced his basic view of nature as the finite expression of the infinite ground of all things. He viewed with horror man's rape and destruction of nature, and he saw this as a logical consequence of the bourgeois spirit. One of his most radical criticisms of capitalism and of modern science was the way in which they misused nature. The former exploited it ruthlessly. The latter viewed nature in a strictly analytical way in order to master and control it. The major sin of both was their narrowly restrictive view or understanding of nature that distorted man as well as nature. Tillich was not opposed to man participating in all the riches and resources of nature, nor did he think it wrong for man to analyze and investigate the structures and content of nature. For that he had great admiration. What he could not abide was the attempt of man to deny anything further to nature, to insist that it was monodimensional, to be controlled, manipulated, exploited, and abused.

Nature was not only something to be loved and appreciated, it was also to be feared. It is a reminder through our very bodies of the boundary on which we live. Thus Tillich was concerned that nature be seen as a finite form through which the infinite was manifest. This led to what he termed a "predominantly aesthetic-meditative attitude" toward nature.[13] In his case, he recalled how his memories and longings were "interlaced with landscapes, with the soil and with weather, with cornfields, and the smell of autumnal potato foliage, with the forms of clouds, with wind, flowers, and woods."[14]

Throughout the diary are descriptions of landscapes, trees, flowers, rain, forests, and weather. This reflects the depth of Tillich's awareness of, and openness to, nature. How many times he speaks of writing on a balcony or in a park! How often he pursued his thinking as he walked in a wood or meadow! Such a concern for nature is deeper than aesthetic, it involves the center of his being. Yet this is not romanticism or pantheism. The divine is encountered through nature, but is not to be confused with nature. The infinite is the ground of nature, and nature points to that depth of reality, but nature is not the divine. Even here there is the problem of possible idolatry, but Paul Tillich never succumbed to that distortion of nature or of the divine.

Perhaps it was his love for the sea that makes absolutely clear both his profound passionate attachment to nature and his distinction between nature and the divine ground. The concrete experience of the sea provided his imagination with the forms necessary so his thought could create concepts of "the absolute as both ground and abyss of dynamic truth, and of the religious essence as the eruption of the eternal into finiteness. . . ."[15] The vision of the sea, infinite in expanse, groundless in depth, gently and eternally rolling in wave upon wave, calm and certain at one moment yet changing into a raging mass of boundless fury, attacking the very heavens that hang low pressing upon it and assaulting the land that seeks to draw back from its fury—this is the vision that kindled Tillich's creative imagination. Even his concept of the boundary drew seminal insight from the sea. Here he saw vividly the infinite bordering on the finite, and he felt both love and fear.

So the diary makes personal or existential Tillich's feeling toward the sea and revals its relationship to his creative thought. His first days at sea reflect all of these dimensions in that relationship—his love for and reveling in the beauty and majesty of the ocean, even the storm and wind, yet also his awaking in terror at the thought of having been left behind in a sinking ship.

His love of nature and the sea in particular is but one more illustration of how Tillich theologized. It was only through concrete experiences and acutely self-conscious participation in all the facets of life that Paul Tillich's imagination could be so kindled that it set fire to his highly original theoretical capacities. That is probably one of the sources of his originality and creativity. He did not simply rearrange theoretical concepts or pursue ever higher levels of abstraction in an attempt to analyze and to explain reality. Experience constantly fructified his imagination which gave an urgency and a relevance to his theological and philosophical conceptualization. Thus he constantly moved between concrete experience and abstract formulation with an actively creative imagination forming the links—providing the boundary between the two.

Just as in nature so in art Tillich found forms that made manifest the divine ground. His love of art was not synthetic or adopted for theological usage. Art was essential for his very being, and he studied it and meditated over it, especially painting, as if his very life depended upon it. In one sense, his life did depend on it for sustenance and for insight into the human predicament—his own and others. Art was a further road to reality along with people and nature. At no point did Tillich want to lose contact with reality. It was almost as if he wished to embrace the whole creation in order that he not miss the presence of the divine. Yet he could not and would not misuse these forms and structures of life by reducing them to mere channels. Each had an autonomy and a givenness of its own dependent upon the ground of being but not identical with that ground.

Tillich's frequent reference in the diary to art, paintings, artists, and museums demonstrates how fully his personal life was bound up with art. He seized every opportunity on the trip to visit and meditate on great works of art both ancient and modern. He demonstrates sensitivity and insight in his comments on buildings, architectural forms, and painting. Most revealing were his comments at the Louvre, "I am now sitting in the Louvre garden beside a fountain, facing a view of the greatest and most magnificent palace in a vanishing world. It is very quiet and the soul fills with silence. At this moment the arc lights come on. I must stop. But once again I know: man creates his world and there is none other— natural or supernatural."[16]

This sounds like a repudiation of his basic view that the finite forms of art express a reference to that which lies beyond them. In fact, his comments at the Louvre are another way of stating the same point. Man in his creative action, in his belief, in his building a culture and a civilization creates his world and there is no other. Only through participating in that world created by man does one experience the ground, the unconditional meaning, which alone gives purpose and signification to that world.

Art can express, can point to ultimate meaning, but it cannot produce it. In *The Religious Situation,* Tillich said, "Art indicates what the character of a spiritual situation is; it does this more immediately and directly than do science and philosophy for it is less burdened by objective considerations. Its symbols have something of a revelatory character while scientific conceptualization must suppress the symbolical in favor of objective adequacy."[17]

It was the immediateness of the symbols of art that appealed to Tillich, for this was one more way for him to counterbalance his strong urge for abstraction and theoretical analysis. Perception of reality through the symbols of art is vastly different from the perception of reality through intellectual concepts. One must use theoretical concepts to write or to talk about reactions to the symbols and forms of art. But these concepts are created and engendered by the reaction of the imagination to the symbols of art. They are not the consequence of a logical analysis of abstract concepts which flow consistently from one to another until a satisfactory explanation is given. Imagination, not precision, is the key to intellectual abstraction. This holds true both for the creation of art and for the initial and primordial response to it. As Tillich said, "The highest form of play and the truly productive abode of imagination is art."[18]

It is interesting to note that in the diary Tillich corrects a statement made earlier in *The Religious Situation*. In that book he had stated, "It is not an exaggeration to ascribe more of the quality of sacredness to a still-life by Cézanne or a tree by Van Gogh than to a picture of Jesus by Uhde."[19] On June 16 Tillich went to the Cézanne exhibit in Paris and gave a detailed reaction to the paintings. Phrases like "mystic pantheism," "breakthrough," "inorganic nature 'lives,' " and "fullness of being" occur.

After viewing Cézanne, Tillich felt compelled to modify his earlier statement about Uhde, which he now felt was a bit unfair. The change was a consequence of two facts. The sheer beauty and charm of the landscape, because of its color, placed the Uhde portrait at a distinct disadvantage, "independent of content." Further, "Cézanne proclaims a mystical devotion to life, and does so with the tools of a very great artist. Uhde proclaims ethical-social devotion with the tools of a minor artist. But basically he, too, is religious."[20] It was impossible for Uhde's work to convey the quality of soundness to the degree of a Cézanne landscape because Cézanne was a much greater artist working with a subject that gave him a distinct advantage over Uhde. Thus the diary exhibits how Tillich drew heavily from art as a basic resource for his theologizing.

If the diary makes evident the way Paul Tillich theologized, nothing documents this more clearly than Tillich in constant discussion and conversation. One is amazed at his voracious appetite for conversation and the almost limitless boundaries of those discussions. In some sense, Tillich appears to have learned more from conversations, at least in later life, than he did from reading. He indicated that he never read great quantities of books, but it is clear that he read the formative books of Western culture and that what he read he mastered. The classics, both ancient and modern, were a part of him, taken into his own creative center. But he did not appear to have dipped very deeply into the stream of books, both fiction and nonfiction, that was flowing from the modern press. In fact, he stated in the diary that "I feel like a barbarian because I never read."[21] He had reached that stage where creative men no longer read books but write them.

It would be a mistake to assume that Tillich was more interested only in writing books, in solitary thought, than in reading them. Conversation replaced reading as the means whereby he engendered new ideas, reacted for or against views of others, developed insights growing out of the confrontation with ideas or concepts, or sharpened perceptions as they emerged. Anybody who conversed with Tillich was aware of having participated in a rare occasion.

Personal encounter and face-to-face confrontation were intergral to his total life as man and as theologian. It provided the concreteness for his existential point of view, and it sustained him in his own humanity. Though he stated on many occasions his belief in, and dependence upon, discussion and debate, his diary demonstrates how fully he lived and thought in that fashion. The diary is one long series of discussions and conversations ranging over a host of essential problems, carried through with an extraordinary number of people representing a variety of professions and positions, and all of this interlaced with personal reactions to the beauties of nature and the stimulation of art.

Three things about conversation were equally important for Paul Tillich and also held true, to a degree, even for lecturing. Human presence and response were highly stimulating for him and called forth his most creative work. He indicated that most of his writing emerged from lectures and addresses that he was invited to give. These public appearances gave him both the greatest anxiety and the greatest joy. There was a communion between the audience and himself that was present in his act of writing even before he appeared before the audience. He wrote for them before he saw them, he anticipated their presence in his preparation for the address. He required an audience to do his most imaginative and inspiring work. The appearance itself, before the audience, actualized the communion, even if there were not questions and answers. People who heard Paul Tillich participated in that communion, the sense of thinking through together common ultimate problems. He brought that to every audience, and they responded to make real the communion he posited by his presence.

Why was this so important for Tillich? He supplied his own answer when he pointed out that discussion and debate are the forms most appropriate for those concerned with existential truth. There one can encounter the truth as it "lives in the immediate self-expression of an experience . . . ." The written word does not have the immediacy nor the impact of the personality of the author behind it. It is one full step removed from the person who wrote it, so it lacks a directness or the urgency of the spoken word.[22] Because the written word lacks the immediacy and directness as well as the presence and power of the author's whole personality, it is not so good a vehicle for confronting existential questions or truth. One is reminded of Luther's insistence that revelation truly occurs when the word is preached and heard in a living communion rather than as it is found written on pages.

It was when the audience had a chance to respond that Tillich was most delighted, for there was the ultimate level of exchange between people. Question and answer, yes and no, formulation of views and rejection or revision of views—all of this occurred in discussion or disputation and provided the dialectics necessary for creative thought and interchange. Paul Tillich called this the "original form of all dialects" and "the most adequate form of my own thinking."[23]

Dialectic marks Tillich's theology at every point and is, in fact, another kind of living on the boundary in thought. It represents a both/and as well as a yes/no, but in either case these must go together. One cannot have only a part of the structure—there is no yes without the no or vice versa. One moves through both of these and stands between them as he holds both in tension. It is the tension between the two, the positing and the rejection before the modification and repositing of the idea, that marked Tillich. How greatly he enjoyed and embodied the dialectical method! Never did it reach its intensity and its dynamics except in the give-and-take of people—an I encountering a Thou. The results could be written down later in the study after careful thought and precise formulation, but the impetus for the idea and creativity of the dialectic was most fully present in the stage of personal confrontation.

That is one reason why for Paul Tillich there was no such thing as a stupid question if it was asked with seriousness. Serious questions, at their depth, were those that involved the very existence of the questioner, they could be questions of ultimate concern. Thus Tillich, in a question-answer situa-

tion, always received a question with the utmost seriousness and frequently rephrased the question in a way that
astonished the one who originally asked it. Invariably, the
way Tillich rephrased the question laid bare what the questioner was really after, but could not adequately formulate.
This was part of Tillich's encounter through dialectic with a
person searching for meaning. Just as he had a genius for
deciphering a myth from a strange religion, so he could
decipher the real meaning of questions asked in discussion.[24]

All these things are revealed by the diary, and in that way
it helps us to understand how Tillich theologized. These
pages sketch out a half year of his life and activity. What is
manifest in these pages is the way a man thought, lived, and
acted. Through the diary one develops a whole new level of
appreciation and understanding of how his theological concepts came to be and why the theologizing moved the way it
did.

Tillich understood himself to be a new kind of scholar,
quite different from his nineteenth-century teachers. He was
different from his teachers, and he did exhibit a new way to
be a scholar. He was not simply an expert fully in control of
all the relevant data in a given discipline—theology. Nor was
he an objective, serene wise man detached from the ebb and
flow of history so that he might speak an eternal word of
truth to mankind caught in the midst of a maelstrom.
He exercised special care in precision and correctness of de-
scription for its own sake but especially to maximize the impact of existential truth. He recognized that he was thrust
directly into history as an intimate part of it, and so the problem of analyzing history—its meaning and content—was fun-
damental for his generation and much more difficult than it
was for his teachers.[25]

To this task he gave himself, and he did not search primarily
for answers that would be true simply in an abstract sense. He
passionately looked for answers that would be existentially

true—for him and for modern man. That is why he had to keep in close contact with his fellow human beings and why he had to probe and search every aspect of their culture and action. Only religion was, by definition, interested in these issues in this particular way. He argued that in religion "theory means something other than philosophical contemplation of being. In religious truth the stake is one's very existence and the question is to be or not to be. Religious truth is existential truth, and to that extent it cannot be separated from practice. Religious truth is *acted*—in accord with the Gospel of St. John."[26]

That is the kind of theologian Paul Tillich was, and his diary demonstrates how he went about being that kind of theologian on a day-to-day basis. He was a human being of enormous complexity involved in culture and society at an astonishing number of points. He lived in, thought about, and reflected upon almost every important facet of contemporary life. This was not done in abstraction but always in relation to people and concrete historical events. Yet in the complexity and sophistication of Tillich and his thought, there was a profound simplicity born of a man who knows where the center of life lies. He did not flee or ignore his tensions nor was he a captive of them. He lived on their boundary.

Just as his central problem was to relate himself to the sacred, to the very ground of being, so his basic theological problem was to see the relation of the sacred to all the structures of creation and forms of culture. He could not bear to see himself, nor any man, cut off from that ground, nor could he bear to see that ground cut off, ignored, or controlled by creation or by culture, the creation of man.

The diary demonstrates that his style of life was the style of his theology. There was no hiatus or inconsistency between them. His life on the boundary was a piece with his theology of the boundary, his love for, and concern with, nature and art were integral to his theological analysis, and his personal involvement with hundreds of people in friendship, discussion, and debate was the grounding for his existential concern and analysis. Paul Tillich's theology was an extension of his life, and his life style reflected his theology. Rarely can this be said of a professor, much less a professor of theology.

April 11

Departure; Hannah and Erdmuthe have come on board
to see me off. Also Lande, the Simonses, and the Goldsteins.
Horkheimer arrives at the last minute with a bottle of cordial.
Then, for a quarter of an hour, I am alone. A sense of
loneliness overcomes me as I watch the crowd of waving,
well-wishing people.

The first lunch aboard ship is unbelievably well prepared.
Red and white wines are set out on the table. After lunch I
am tired and decide to stretch out on my bunk.

After a short rest I go back up on deck: we are out in the
open sea by now, which is very calm and foggy. We pass the
Ambrose light ship; it emits fog signals. I take a long leisurely
stroll around the entire deck which has as yet not been partitioned off according to classes. It is quite empty. I take a cup
of coffee in the social room.

Then I begin work on my lectures.

By dinnertime everyone has been assigned a place in the
dining room, and I sit next to a young composer who has
just won a prize and has had his work performed by the
Philharmonic orchestra.

Across the table from me, a nice elderly lady who tells me
she was born in France. After dinner I take another stroll
around the deck. There are phosphorescent marine animals
afloat in the wake of the ship. I point them out to two sis-

ters, Jewish girls from Chicago who are on their way to Moscow. They are going to visit their married sister there, via an Intourist trip for which they have saved. We walk agreeably about Russia. Later I have a chess lesson. Early to bed, after putting away my things. Wonderful, profound sleep.

April 12; Easter Sunday

I am awakened by the furious pitching of the ship. Take two Vasano capsules. They produce a dry sensation in the stomach, but do prevent seasickness. Warm, moist, sunless Gulf Stream weather.

I settle down in a deck chair on the upper deck, by myself, and continue working on those lectures. By now the three classes of the ship have been partitioned off. My favorite walk on the tourist deck is toward a pilot bridge at the stern. This bridge commands the most sweeping view of the ocean—from left to right, from right to left. There is not much sun—a strange atmosphere for Easter Sunday. Later in the afternoon the two girls from Chicago, who are traveling third class, manage to turn up in first.

There is a lavish Easter dinner—twelve courses and a huge Easter egg. The composer, my former neighbor at the table has disappeared. I am alone with the lady from France. We labor at our French conversation. I understand everything she says, but at first am unable to utter a single French word myself. It is an amazing psychological experience: the English words—my new language—have completely blocked my French. Only with tremendous, almost physical effort can I get out any French at all.

Later there is a dance. The two girls from Chicago—their name is Goldmann—have returned from their excursion in first class. I dance one dance with each girl. Then I spend a long time on deck. A warm wind is blowing and the sea is full of phosphorescence. Every day we lose almost an hour as the clock is moved ahead.

April 13

I get up early. The ship rolls heavily from side to side. Again I have recourse to Vasano. It rains and a sou'wester is blowing. The ocean is magificent.

After breakfast I return to my cabin. Though I had closed the window firmly, water has sprayed in and all my shirts and several notebooks are wet. The steward closes the iron outer portholes.

The sun comes out for awhile, and it suddenly gets very warm. Later the sun disappears again, the storm increases. In the dining room, bottles and glasses have been placed in special wooden trays with holes to hold them in place.

After lunch I take a nap in my dark cabin. Later, some aimless conversation; later still, I do some work on deck in full view of a splendid warm-stormy sea. Toward evening the sun breaks through the clouds once more.

I encounter an Austrian acquaintance of Heinz Ziegler's who had once come to see us in Frankfurt. He lives in New York and is a fashion illustrator.

After dinner I get some work done in my cabin. Later I have an extremely successful chess lesson. A starry night—the first since this voyage began.

April 14

The weather has improved. At breakfast I am called upon to interpret between two ladies, one American and the other French. By and large, though, I have not met many people. This is not a very interesting crowd. I enjoy watching two peroxide blonde "flappers" with ditto mother; a Cuban-looking family. I spend many hours alone, in my solitary chair on the upper deck, working. The people in first class are said to be even duller—according to Ziegler's Austrian friend. The third class, with several Russia-bound travelers, somehow sounds more promising.

By noon the sky has turned completely blue; the sun burns down, the sea is vast and blue. I work on my lectures for "History and the Kingdom of God." In the afternoon I discover that I have a sunburn as a result of working in the sun for hours. At dinner I am happy to find that my block against the French language is beginning to dissolve at last.

Back on deck after an hour and a half of work. The sea and sky have once more changed completely. A howling southeasterly storm has sprung up; the night is pitch black. There is a salty spray and the wind whistles in the masts. Every evening from 9:00 to 10:00 a "horse race" takes place on board. Tonight, for a change, the six most beautiful girls are "running" in it. Then from 10:00 to 11:00 there is dance music, but not many people seem to want to dance. I am off to bed. From 10:30 the time has jumped to 11:30 by a twist of the clock hand.

The porthole is still closed in my cabin. Outside, the elements are in a fearful uproar.

April 15

I awake after a bad night. I suddenly am afraid that I have been left behind on a sinking ship. For a second I experience true mortal terror. I switch on the light and take a sip of water. Then I fall back into a light sleep, close to the storm.

This morning the sea is white and raging. On one side of my favorite bridge the wind blows so fiercely that it throws me back. The ship rolls only very slightly. Ragged clouds . . . cold air. At lunch there are many empty places in the dining room. After a short nap I spend a long time on the upper deck. The ocean is splendid, all black and white with gray clouds above, a gray-blue wake, foaming whitecaps. Later I read Heimann in the lounge, while sipping coffee and listening to a concert. Toward evening I return to the deck, where I meet the wife of an American doctor.

31

The storm continues with unabating force. At dinner I speak a great deal of French while enjoying a bottle of real sauterne, delicate as a poem. There follows a long evening in the smoking room while next door they are having their horse race and dance. Once again, as in the old days in Berlin, I find myself working in cafés.

I get into a conversation with the doctor's wife's sister. She turns out to be Communist. She intends to study in Russia. We get into an argument. She is convinced that a Communist victory is imminent, even in America. She rejects Niebuhr's teachings.

In the middle of our chess game we are being invaded by the *jeunesse dorée* from the first class. They want to dance. All are extremely good-looking, quite a different breed from the middle-class people all around us. The first-class passenger list is full of titled names which seems strange, coming from America.

April 16

Again I have experienced that oppressive terror during the night, though not quite so bad as the first time. In the morning the sun is out and the ocean is radiantly blue. I work in the sun all day on my lectures for a "Philosophy of History." The ship rolls continuously; but I only need one Vasano.

Baron Ignace d'Ephrussi (this is Ziegler's friend whose name I have grasped, at long last) and I observe the uncanny speed with which time passes due to the fact that we are robbed of an hour every day.

At night there is an elaborate gala dinner, the big farewell ceremony. We drink the last of the sauterne. The Misses Goldmann invite me to join them in third class. They have a very comfortable room for dancing and drinking there. The walls are painted. Dance music is supplied by a radio.

There are extraordinary people in third class. An old Jew with a skullcap, sitting in one corner, is responsible for the kosher meals on board. There are some towering Italians. And two Canadian social workers, one a Russian girl by birth. They are both going to Russia. There is also a New York family en route to Russia. The mother, who works for a German immigrant committee, dresses in Russian style. As I arrive, a big cotton snowball fight is in progress. I dance with everyone, and enjoy myself ten times more than in the tourist class. Here are intellectuals, proletarians, Communists, Jews.

At the same time there is a gala dinner and gala night in first class. Our "flappers," who, as it turns out, are chorus girls, have been invited to this event, and so have some other young beauties. Anyone who refuses to believe in the existence of class distinctions should have to answer this question: "Did you ever cross the Atlantic Ocean on one of the big liners?" Nowhere else in the world are the different classes to be found so close together—and nowhere else are the contrasts more obvious. A large percentage of the third-class passengers are going to Moscow.

April 17

The last day on board. I have changed some money, got my luggage ready, finished the lectures in bright sunlight with a blue sea all around me. The trip has really been too short. I should have had two weeks in order to get everything properly prepared.

Red wine and French food are balm to one's stomach, even to one that is threatened by seasickness. And everything was so light and excellent that it would have been a shame to abstain.

Unfortunately, on this trip the American element predominated over the French. But my French conversation has grown steadily more fluent. This voyage was like a week's

Easter vacation at a big hotel on the water, with lots of work, rest, few people to talk to, and a beautiful view of the ocean.

As we get closer to Europe, the old Continent takes on greater reality in my mind, and the apocalyptic dreams of shipwreck and drowning cease. We pass other ships now, after six days of not seeing a single one. The ocean here is almost too blue, cold, northwesterly. I pack and go to sleep—will be awakened at 5:00 A.M. tomorrow.

April 18

Awaken at 4:45. A quick breakfast, then passport inspection. They ask me whether I will definitely not seek permanent employment over here.

Up on deck: I see Plymouth Bay in the cold, reddish morning sun; it reminds me of my first arrival in New York. But the landscape is wonderful—with real European forests!

A motor launch takes us ashore. Then on to London by train. The ride goes through lovely rolling country, full of trees in bud and masses of primroses. The most exciting thing to see is the intense green of the meadows. I ask some Americans how this landscape strikes them, as they are seeing it for the first time. They say: "So clean, and so natural." It is certainly different from the American landscape that has been ravaged by technology, and also from the forbidding wilderness to be found in many nonindustrial regions of America.

The trains here run incredibly fast. Ours does not make a single stop along the way.

At the station are Mrs. Niebuhr and a nice young clergyman named Lister, Oldham's assistant. We have a typically English lunch together in the railway station restaurant. It is very different from the light French cuisine.

Then we cross London, riding on the roof of a bus. Everything looks very small and old world to me; even

London Bridge seems unimpressive compared to Brooklyn Bridge.

From Liverpool Station I leave for Norwich, capital of England's easternmost county. Thus I have today traversed all of England from the extreme southwest to the extreme east—in a matter of five hours by train. So small is this country whose political decisions affect the whole world!

Everywhere there is the same rich green; there are trees and bushes; flowers; villages. I feel sad because, while this is Europe, my home—it is *not* Germany, and therefore not really my home.

At the station, in Norwich, I am met by Oldham with a magnificent automobile driven by Lord Lothian's chauffeur. We get in, and are whisked along a winding country road at a speed of 75 miles per hour.

Around 6:30 we arrive at Blickling Hall, one of the most famous country seats of British nobility. Dutch Renaissance, dating back to 1620. I am immediately taken in hand by the butler and two manservants. One of them takes my suitcase in order to unpack it. For this purpose I must leave the room, so that he can have a free hand. Later I will find all my things beautifully arranged and distributed.

Downstairs, Oldham shows me two marvelous paintings by Holbein, a Van Dyck, a Canaletto, etc. On the staircase stands a wooden statue of Anne Boleyn who was born in a house nearby. There is also a huge wall tapestry, a gift from Catherine II to one of Lord Lothian's ancestors who was ambassador to St. Petersburg. There are several portraits by Lawrence and many other ancestral portraits all bearing an unmistakable family resemblance to the present Lord, the last, childless, heir to the house of Lothian. I meet Lord Lothian himself before dinner—he is in evening clothes, of course—a powerful man who would look very well wearing armor. He is a member of the House of Lords and he knows everyone.

Sherry is served before dinner and all sorts of wine during the meal. I sit next to Lord Lothian and we talk about democracy and free trade. After dinner we talk about the Oxford conference. Lord Lothian is chairman. The others are: Oldham; Pastor Menn from Andernach, an old Religious Socialist; Schoenfelt and Ehrenstrom from the Conference Bureau for the Preparation of the Oxford Protestant World Conference; the president of the French Protestant Church Union; one professor each from Oxford and Cambridge; a junior member of the Foreign Office, the Secretary of the Stockholm Conference, a professor of law from Leipzig. The problem: Church and nation.

In the evening we have a practical discussion of the book that is to be written in preparation for the Oxford conference.

April 19

After midnight last night I sank into my huge bed—my head in a whirl. There is a beautiful brocade wall rug at my head, a flickering fireplace at my feet.

This morning I am awakened by a manservant with tea and sandwiches and warm water. Downstairs, a self-service breakfast is laid out. From there I walk out into the princely park.

Outside my window lies a meadow that could have been painted by Böcklin; full of hyacinths of many colors. Farther back there is a stand of ancient, indescribably noble pine trees. On the other side, where the moat used to be, there is now a sunken garden with camellias, and beyond that, a broad swath of lawn bordered by boxwood hedges trimmed in French style.

I find that Menn exactly shares my views on the situation in Germany. From 10:00 to 1:00—discussion. I give a résumé of my interpretation of the European situation, and speak out against the English appeasement policy.

After lunch Lord Lothian invites me to join him in an

hour-long walk during which he explains his own theory to me: the Western democracies are to protect themselves by keeping aloof from the quarrels of European dictators. Germany is to be appeased and allowed to gain supremacy over Central Europe. France and Belgium will thus be safeguarded.

In the evening the Foreign Office representative tells me that he considers Lothian's theory untenable. He feels that Germany must never be allowed to gain that much power. He adds that England is always politically paralyzed when faced with real fanaticism because the English imagination cannot grasp a situation that allows of no compromise.

In the debates over the upcoming Oxford conference there are two distinctly different viewpoints: the Lutheran-German and the Anglo-Saxon. I feel that I have somehow come to stand on the boundary between the two.

After the debate I walk through the park alone. I hear, for the first time in two and a half years, that unforgettable concert of bird song. I meet Lord Lothian who is also walking alone. As he puts it: he is seeking respite in nature from human problems. He shows me some pheasants and dozens of deer. None of these animals are ever hunted.

After dinner we have some informal conversation. Then early to bed. The Lothian library, which was bought from a French cardinal, is housed in a long, narrow hall. A Clouet hangs in the study.

April 20

Awakened early by the famous cup of tea. Outside, it is snowing. The manservant helps me pack.

At breakneck speed through rain and snow to the railroad station. I have breakfast on the train, then I doze a little, and talk with some fellow passengers.

In London both Niebuhr ladies are at the station. We take a bus ride through the city to the National Gallery. We visit the Italian wing. I can hardly breathe, am almost in tears. These museum walls are irradiated by the same beauty that illuminted our trip to Italy. Here I go from Uccello to Leonardo, to Raphael, to the primitives.

In the German wing I run into the two sisters I had met on the ship. Later I have lunch with an English friend of Barbara's. We eat in an old city restaurant with open charcoal grill and Dickens' illustrations on the walls. Next, a brief visit to the uncanny Tower after which I recuperate in a tea room. Then I am off to the conference.

I read my lectures on the "Philosophy of History," which seem to make a strong impression on everyone. Copies are being sent around today. After the reading there is a discussion, then supper, then more discussions.

I am taken to visit an international students' home with many Indians and Negroes. At ten o'clock Lister whisks me off to his parsonage in London N. E. We ride a bus through long dark streets composed of one-story houses. After New York, they look like shacks.

The parsonage house has been donated by Eton College. I had suggested stopping on the way for a glass of port in a pub. Instead, Lister calls for his Anglican vicar (first pastor), who promptly arrives with two bottles of fine cordial which we manage to finish between us, sitting and talking until midnight in the parsonage office. They are wonderful, cultured men.

I wake up in the middle of the night thinking I am still on board ship. Have to get up and look out the window to convince myself that this is not so.

April 21

Up early, I ride to the conference. The discussion goes on till noon. Mr. Espy comes up to me and asks me whether I can take part in the International Conference of Youth Leaders in Lausanne this coming September. I leave the question open. Ursula Niebuhr arrives with a friend, a German-English girl. We eat at the Tate and make fun of the Rossetti period.

The two ladies and I have to go to Mr. Benn's for tea. Mr. Benn was the Labour Government's Secretary of State for India. I expatiate on my views about Europe and England's failure. He becomes quite excited but still agrees with me on many things. He feels strongly that England must not cede any of her colonies to Germany.

Afterward I pay a short visit to the Warburg Institute of Hamburg, which is now located in London. There I meet Sasel with Mrs. Bing, and advise them to stay in England instead of going to New York.

Oldham awaits me at Victoria Station. We take the train to his country house, through lovely rolling country. He has a beautiful garden. Unfortunately, it is ice-cold and snowing. The only warm spot in the house is the fireplace.

At supper we are joined by a middle-aged lady who works for Oldham and who has traveled clear across Central Africa with another woman as her only companion. Also present is Oldham's married niece who makes her home on the Gold Coast.

After dinner we have coffee beside the fireplace. Later Oldham and I have a quiet personal talk near the fire.

They have put me up in a nearby house which is a combination inn and antique shop. The old Oldhams walk over there with me; she is armed with a hot water bottle for me. Now I am here, sitting beside the cold fireplace, surrounded by antiques, sipping a glass of port, writing this. Today I had my first letter from Hannah.

April 22

Up early and into the city with Oldham. I make a number of phone calls at his office. In half an hour I have disposed of my entire day.

First, to the National Gallery where I discover a Michelangelo and several Raphaels. Many French and English painters. One should really have at least a week here to see it all.

Later, in a tea room, I meet Dr. Adler. He had been arrested in the Kuessel, then went to Prague, and is now working at a country school in England. His writings appear in Germany under a pseudonym. His work is greatly appreciated there, because—as he puts it—they have only idiots left. He tells me that Claire behaved extremely well; that the Pincusses want to go to Russia, and the Loewenfelds are en route to Syria.

To the telegraph office where Berthe Grossbard expects me. We have lunch together. She has grown older and more mature and is enjoying a great deal of success. She is extremely nice and warm toward me. She takes me to the Lyceum Club where she is now a big wheel. She has struggled valiantly and energetically. She left Italy because of the war and hopes to make her career in London. After we part, I stroll through the amusement section by myself.

At four o'clock I return to the same tea room where I now meet S. She lives here under an assumed name with a man she would like to marry but cannot, because of technical difficulties with passports, etc. We walk through St. James's Park to Westminster Abbey. She, too, has become older and more mature. She is "working," has seen the Useners and been annoyed by Herrmann's attitude. She does not believe in P.'s suicide; has become suspected herself; feels cool toward Mannheim and Loewe, who reject her "work."

At six, at the same tea room again, I meet Frau v. Bock who begs me to look after Elisabeth. She tells me that her father has not yet been reinstituted. And that Erhardt, unfortunately, has became very careful—like Elisabeth. She tells me that the secretaries at the German legation are treated badly; that Ribbentrop caused Hoetsch to have a heart attack. She talks of suitcases standing packed and ready after the Germans had marched into the Rhineland; about a report from the Bureau of Statistics that only 53% voted for Hitler. She says that none of the people she personally knows voted for him. To listen to her, nobody at all is for him.

We have dinner together. She leaves at 8:30, after which I see S. again. She wants me to meet her friend, but we cannot arrange it because I have to call for Oldham at the Athenaeum Club at 9:45.

Back to the country with Oldham. We walk through the starry night to my lonely farmhouse.

April 23

Sleep late. I wake up with a sore throat due to the icy cold in my ancient, unheated attic room. I fight down an incipient cold with hot lemon juice and aspirin all through the day.

I give Oldham a résumé of my theory of mass reintegration; of heresy and its rejection by the Synod; of the formation of program and religious orders. He is profoundly impressed.

We take a long walk in sunny, warm, spring weather and listen to the cuckoo and many other birds. Lovely wide vistas open before us. Everything is very green. Oldham says that he finds my idea about *religious orders* a thousand times more important than the whole Oxford conference for which he is working day and night.

In the afternoon we visit Sir Walter Moberly, a nobleman of low rank—a "Ford" among the English aristocracy. Above him are Baronet, Baron, Viscount, Earl, Marques, Duke. This gives you an idea of how high up Lothian is—he is a Marquess —on this scale. All ranks above Knight are Peers and must be addressed as Lord. A Knight is addressed as Sir. All this, which seems funny to us, has no political significance at all, but tremendous social importance. It is a part of that "conformity" that so impresses Adolf.

Sir Walter was in bed with a sprained ankle. His is a beautiful country house with a fine park full of magnificent old trees; a wonderful view. I remark later that I wish one of our best works could be as fine as the tree Sir Walter sees from his bed.

He is a former Vice-Chancellor of Manchester and is also a philosopher with an excellent background in theology. He and I get along very well. He asks me to give his regards to the Loewes.

At dinner we are joined by Nash, a young clergyman, who maps out the next evening, which he has arranged, for me.

Later I sit by the fire with Oldham, and something like personal warmth begins to grow up between us. He says he wants to introduce me to the English public, and he wants to see me again in Paris and Geneva. A few times, when I try to take my suitcase off his hands, he assures me quite earnestly that no Englishman could possibly allow his guest to carry a suitcase.

Then to bed.

April 24

I pack, call a car, and go to London alone. Take a taxi from Charing Cross to Paddington Station where I finally pick up my two big suitcases that have been waiting there almost a week. By taxi to the Red Court Hotel where the Mannheims are staying. However, they are out at the moment.

At last I have a real room where I can keep all my luggage, change my clothes, etc. Of course, there is no heat except for a gasburner which I turn on immediately.

Wearing my black suit, I go to see an earl. We have lunch with Ursula Niebuhr and an editor of the *Economist*.

Having arrived too early, I decide to pay a quick visit to the Victoria and Albert Museum for Arts and Crafts. There I chance upon an exhibit of silhouettes by Lotte Reininger who once did a silhouette of me at Hiddensee. I still have it among my things.

The Earl's wife is a writer. It turns out that she and I both crossed the Atlantic on the *Paris*—tourist class—but did not get to know each other on board.

We discuss English foreign policy. Everyone instantly agrees with my criticism. There is an atmosphere of total confusion and despair. The man from the *Economist* feels that English politics can come to no good so long as the country is run by dotards. He is sharply against Lord Lothian's pro-German attitude. But he has a utopian idea that it is possible to create a collective security system based on an exact definition of the "attacker." He feels, though, that at the moment this, too, is hopeless because of the situation in England.

In talking to the Countess I learn that she has been lecturing in America—on the woman's question. She tells me that K. has called her a liar, which has infuriated her. She assures me that she has tried to be absolutely fair, and to use only German statistical material. She thinks K. must be an agent of the German government. Yesterday I asked A. about this, since it was he, after all, through whom I met K. He shares the Countess' suspicion, and he also thinks that K. may be working for the Communists as well, and also for K. He says that this is the way all informers work.

Later Ursula and I go to Oldham's by car. After she leaves, Oldham and I attend a settlement meeting. There are many intellectuals present. Afterwards we have tea at the house of a very distinguished lady—beautiful, despite her gray hair. Oldham presents my ideas to a roomful of fashionable young people. After he has spoken, I answer questions from the group.

Next, Nash and Lister take me to the P.E.N. Club. We go by tube: the tube is a series of long, underground conduits, very deep down. There is a separate tube for each track. It is all very loud, hot, and fast. The club, which is devoted to planning research, is near St. James's Park. I feel that I am really in Europe here. The whole thing reminds me of the Tiergartenstrasse or the Taunus-Anlage.

Dinner is 7:00. About thirty people attend, among them many leading figures. After dinner we settle down in a wide semicircle around the fireplace. I speak on mass disintegration and meaninglessness—the causes of National Socialism. I criticize England's pacificism severely. My speech gives rise to a debate that continues until 10:30. What seems to have impressed the listeners most deeply are my remarks about the tragic and ethical elements in the destiny of nations.

At 11:00 I meet Dada Langer. She is now a British subject, thanks to a marriage to an Englishman. We take a long leisurely walk through the streets and watch the theaters let out: many men in dinner jackets, ladies in fur coats but without stockings. Many prostitutes.

We try to get a glass of beer in a restaurant, but have to order sandwiches, since they refuse to serve beer alone. Ten minutes later we get thrown out anyway, because it is now midnight and the place is closing. In a Lyon's Corner House, a sort of giant Aschinger, they don't serve any alcoholic beverages at that hour.

Dada Langer is not happy in London—a feeling she shares with many. She complains that the distances are too great. For instance, she has been able to see S. only once. She has met Teddy only once—by accident—in the street. She works very hard and would like to go to the colonies, or to New York. Still, she looks much better now than she did in Frankfurt. She has been to see Steinrath and Gerti Siemsen, and says that both are in bad shape. Both are lethargic—their vitality gone. Dada Langer talks about her own escape from Germany by way of a cemetery near Saarbrücken. As soon as she had crossed the border into France, she went to the first French governor she could find. He tested her—to see if she really was a student—by asking: "Where is Professor Tillich?" Answer: "In New York." Correct. ". . . Professor Wertheimer?" "Oh his way to New York." Correct. This was all the proof he asked. Like most refugees, she does not feel at ease in London, except when she is in the company of a few Germans she knows.

I go to bed tired.

April 25

Packing my bags until eleven o'clock. I am taking only my briefcase and one suitcase for this week's trip, and will leave the blue and brown traveling bags in London.

To Manchester; it is a three-and-a-half-hour train ride through the garden that is called England. On this train you are immediately seated at dining car tables—in third class. Good, inexpensive lunch, accompanied by good conversation.

Adolf and Dora await me at the station and take me to their house by car. They have a big house which stands in a meadow. Inside their fireplace there is a German iron stove which provides an agreeable temperature. Both children have turned out very good-looking; Bea is much more attractive than she was in Frankfurt; Adolf has a strong, rounded face. We all agree instantly, overwhelmingly, on the subject of English politics. After coffee we take a stroll through the nearby park. Everything here is so beautiful and European, even though Manchester is an awful factory town with much rain and fog. We talk a great deal about various friends.

I explain my basic ideas about the religious order. Loewe feels very much alone. He lives as if he has a sinecure, with few actual duties. Many birds sing in the parks and gardens around here.

Late to bed, very tired.

April 26

I wake up happy to have a few quiet days ahead. It is Sunday morning: I take a stroll through the park. At the park

46

pond grownups and children sail their large toy boats with incredible passionate absorption. Adolf—after watching them for awhile—talks about the English type of conformity which impresses him profoundly. We discuss its causes and whether it would be possible to bring about a socialist conformity, a historically developed uniform attitude, beyond all tensions and conflicts.

During the afternoon and evening we work on the program with very fruitful results. We abandon the idea that the religious order is *our* task. I agree with Adolf—as with no other person—on all essential program points. He feels *very* positive toward Russia.

Late—tired—to bed.

April 27

Theological discussion after my sermon and lecture on Protestantism: "New Wine in Old Bottles."

I go for a walk with Gerhard Meyer and his family. We discuss Russia versus America. In the afternoon—a long stroll through Spath Park which makes me feel as if I were in Dresden.

Debate over the program. Late into the evening with program notes. Ulenspiegel sherry. Bea dreams about my father.

April 28

At the university Adolf reads a brilliant seminar on "Expansion and Reorientation" before five unresponsive students. There is a huge poster announcing my lecture.

After Adolf's lecture we visit a most remarkable Gothic cathedral. Main points of interest: a coffered ceiling, and the tombstone of an ancestor of Moseley, the Fascist leader who is now completely out of the limelight.

Chetham Hospital: a former parsonage with an old library, which has been made into a school for boys. Even boys from proletarian families can get as far as Oxford from here.

Next, a visit to the slums which date back to the beginning of the nineteenth century. Aesthetically interesting streets composed of one-story houses which contain small flats with comparatively good furniture. Every street. Women in shawls; completely emaciated bodies. There is a sense of hopelessness, caused by unemployment which, in turn, is due to England's loss of the Indian cotton market. The younger people are being relocated in southern industrial areas. The remaining population gives a resigned impression—unaggressive. At the same time there is some sort of festivity going on—a government anniversary is being celebrated.

I spend some time preparing my lecture. At seven o'clock, dinner with Canon Cheetham and his wife, plus about twelve students of theology.

My lecture: on the religious situation in Germany. There is a large audience—and tremendous applause. During the discussion period I receive a number of questions with detectable Nazi tendencies. At the same time there is a strong sense of "sympathy with the emigrant." After the lecture the Loewes have arranged a reception at which the Stocks, Sir Simon, the Sinclairs, and others are present. The talk is mainly about education.

Sherry and sleep.

April 29

The Manchester Guardian carries a good article on my lecture of last night. Several people call up and tell me that it has made a very strong impression. Is it the subject—or the speaker's "nice personality"?

Long discussion of Adolf's book, *The Dynamic of Cycles*.

In the afternoon we visit the new housing project with the Stocks. The core of the project is a medieval country house that has gone through repeated renovations, during the Elizabethan and later periods. This house stands in a magnificent park. Sir Simon had bought the place and donated it to the city, which added some beautiful, solid project houses. The whole thing reminds me of Britz.

Adolf and I work hard until late into the night.

April 30

I must pack and go to the bank, and see the Meyers; one last stroll with Adolf. I strongly agree with his decision to stay. At noon I depart for Edinburgh. The train traverses an industrial landscape first, later the entire countryside around us turns into one big garden. Bay of the Irish Sea. Cattle, stone fences, hills.

On the way to Lancaster I see snowcapped mountains and willow trees still gray with leaf buds. Only in Europe is there such a blue spring sky with such white clouds. Hannah's second and third letters have reached me by now.

I have a talk with an old white-haired Scot, a type clear out of Shakespeare. The countryside turns bleak. We are now in Scotland and surrounded by many mountains which all seem very high and forbidding. I am put in mind of the wonderful Dickensian secondhand bookstore where we bought the works of Locke and Hume.

Treeless, round-topped mountains. Entrances to mine shafts. As we approach Edinburgh, the landscape broadens. The mountains recede toward the background. Theatrical-looking sheep graze in the meadows.

At the Edinburgh station the Baillies' son recognizes me instantly. He and Erdmuthe used to have snowball fights in the Quadrangle. We drive into the marvelous garden of the Baillies' house. The garden has southern needle trees and many flowers. In the house, an excellent room has been assigned to me. Mrs. Baillie is in London.

After a walk through the garden, I dress for dinner, which is a banquet in my honor for the faculty and invited guests.

Baillie and I walk through the ancient streets. All the

houses are made of fieldstone. Many are several stories high. Once, these were the palaces of the nobility. They are slum dwellings now.

An ancient stairway leads up to the faculty hall, where about twenty professors are assembled. All are either in dinner jackets or clerical dress, like Baillie.

I am seated at the Dean's right, next to Patterson, an old systematic theologian. At the end of the dinner the Dean welcomes me officially. Then we move to the fireplace where we sit in a semicircle and coffee is served. Mackintosh and I talk about Kaehler.

Later I deliver a long, completely impromptu speech. I pose three questions: (1) How can we arrive at a principle of reintegration? (2) Is the life o nations tragic or ethical-progressive in character? (3) Is the idea of a "holy nation" an idea which can be turned into fact?

In the discussion which follows, points (1) and (3) get the maximum of attention.

Baillie and I spend an hour together afterward, talking and drinking red wine. He says that my address was "fascinating because of the strange character of your thinking." Next day the Dean says that it was the most interesting evening they ever had in that hall. I am to put the questions and answers in writing and send them to him.

The bed I sleep in is marvelous.

May 1

A sunny, hazy morning filled with loud birdsong. Tea in bed, then breakfast.

To town, alone. I visit the castle I had seen beautifully illuminated the night before when it had been lighted without even the slightest hint of bad taste. A wonderful view in all directions. St. Giles Cathedral has a steeple shaped like the Scottish crown. Inside, the usual Puritan devastations. The intersecting vaults are made of beautiful dark gray stone.

Down to the National Gallery; it is small but has some excellent things, only everything is too crowded. I return through Princes Street which has a view of the castle and the mountains. After lunch I go to give my lecture.

A large audience has gathered in yesterday's hall. The Dean's introduction strongly emphasizes emigration. Afterward there is much applause and a "vote of thanks" from Baillie. The ovation makes me feel obliged to tone things down in my reply. I say how much my having been accepted into the English-American world has meant to me in terms of a revival of my will to work. Both yesterday and today there are many magnificent heads to be seen in the hall, reminding me of the best German conferences—even surpassing those in some respect . A great many come up to thank me.

In Patterson's car to the palace of Mary Queen of Scots. We visit the rooms; her secret supper chamber, her bedroom, etc. All very moving. Then Professor Porteous, a former student of Karl Barth's, leads us up the 850-foot mountain called Arthur's Seat—because it is shaped like a lion; King Arthur is said to have ridden a lion. I marvel at this group of completely untouched grassy hills right in the center of town; neither the town, nor the army, nor privite interests has laid claim to this bit of unspoiled nature. We have a good view of the town, the mountains, and the ocean.

After changing our clothes, we go to the club where, once more, we enter the small hall. The director of the library tells me about the ancient clan feuds which to this day make it impossible for a member of one clan to allow a descendant of an enemy clan to do even a typing job, or repair a pair of shoes for him.

Lots of good wine at dinner. Afterward, an intense christological discussion with Mackintosh and a pedagogical discussion with the head of Scotland's most distinguished public school—what Eton is to England: not a public school in our sense, but a very expensive country boarding school. I walk home through a moonlit spring night.

101435

May 2

Up early to take the boy, Ian to the Forth Bridge. It is a wonderful, hazy, sunny day. The birds are jubilant. We take the train across the bridge, which is sixty years old and still has a grandiose air, with its gigantic tubular piers. We walk back to the ferry, then cross over on the ferry, alongside the bridge. Back by train, through masses of flowering Scotch broom.

We go to the Edinburgh docks and ride through them by car, which delights the boy. Two glimpses of the open North Sea—the native ocean of my heart. Over there, a little off to one side, to the southwest, lies Germany! Kampen!

At lunch, a gathering of professors of philosphy. I have an intense talk with Smith about the second phase of Schelling. Then I must pack and leave for Manchester. Always that same hazy, sunny weather, devoid of shrill colors. The sun is a red ball high in the sky. Melancholy mood.

At the Manchester station Adolf receives me "like a bride." For two intense hours we walk back and forth through the streets; then to my sleeping car.

May 3

Bad night in the sleeping car from Manchester to London. In London, as the train stands in the station, they wake me with a cup of tea. I leave the train at 7:30 and go to the hotel where I find Julia Mannheim, and later Karl. Both are enormously glad to see me; "overjoyed," as they put it.

Breakfast; at the table next to mine there are some Russians, men and women from the Embassy. I meet an architect from Darmstadt, a friend of the Mannheims, whose house we had once visited.

A room with a fire burning in the fireplace awaits me at the Red Court Hotel. We talk about Europe and America; report on the program outline. Very good talk. Julia looks a bit older and more tired; Karl is almost completely unchanged. We are on intimate "du" (thou) terms right away.

After twelve o'clock I am to visit Pollock who is sick in bed at the Russell Hotel. I have lunch with Mandelbaum whom the Institute has commissioned to prepare an analysis of the economic situation in Europe. He tells me how ill at ease he felt in Paris because of the hostility of the French toward foreigners.

Then, my visit with Pollock who had contracted fish poisoning in Paris. Leisurely walk around Russell Square. European feelings.

I lie down in my room, and the Mannheims come and we have a bedside discussion.

Tea, Russell Square Park with separate key. Mannheim tells me about his professional problems. We have a good dinner at the hotel.

I am off to see Frau v. Bock and her friend, Frl. v. Fleck, a very intelligent, pretty young secretary who works at the Embassy. She has done some work for the counterintelligence division and tells many grisly stories, including one about three noblewomen who worked as spies and who were told by a fortuneteller that one of them would be beheaded.

She hates the Nazis and refuses to have anything to do with Embassy officials. Complains about her loneliness.

I leave early: it is Sunday and there are no more subways after eleven o'clock.

Wine and conversation at Mannheim's bed.

My hotel room is very pleasant.

May 4

After a leisurely breakfast I telephone Margy Wichert, then walk to Oldham's office, to the post office, to make some telephone calls, etc.

At 12:45 Schairer calls for me at the hotel and we drive to Golders Green. He is very nice, explains his own idea of my religious-order idea to me.

53

Mrs. Schairer is in slacks and blouse, looks fresh, but has aged. They have a charming house with garden. After lunch we take coffee outside on the lawn. Schairer has completely broken with the Nazis, but he openly and wistfully longs to be in Germany. His wife is strongly anti-Nazi, paints a horrifying picture of Germany. The youth problem: fifteen million young people working for rearmament in Europe. Radicalization and disappointment of German youth. Institute for Youth Studies. The tragic self-destruction of the older generation—taking one wrong step after another. Their talk with Schacht, who is completely subservient to Hitler. I talk with Mrs. Schairer about Elsa—Elsa Branstrom; Gerda Schairer had written about Elsa in a book; and Elsa had been hurt by her remarks. She feels quite innocent, but the whole thing depresses her.

Sybille Dreyfuss arrives, now happy as Mrs. Moholy-Nagy. She has greatly changed: her hair is now natural, her face round and motherly, her figure full. She has two children. Gropius and Schoens are in London, too; and so is Dreyfuss who works in motion pictures. She is completely out of touch with him, but sees Teddy from time to time.

We walk to her house and have tea on the lawn. It is a very modern house, with many abstract paintings by Moholy. Everyone advises him to go to America.

The Schairers take me back to my hotel; then the Mannheims and I visit the London School of Economics; ancient, crooked, crumbling houses and one huge modern building. Wooden stairs; old, worm-eaten beams.

I meet Dr. Cahn-Freud, formerly a judge, who worked with Sinsheimer right after Sinsheimer's release from prison. A good-looking man.

A phone call from Anita Lothar: she and her husband have moved to London.

A short visit to the Parthenon Frieze at the British Museum. Then to see Canon Barry in the cloisters of Westminster Abbey. We walk through ancient, beautiful cloisters to his apartment. His wife, who once lived at Union Seminary, is very nice.

The Barrys' guests include: the Secretary to the Archbishop of Canterbury (who looks like a papel nuncio); the headmaster of Westminster Public School; two very distinguished old theologians whose names escape me. The hall and surrounding sections of the Abbey are sixteenth century. Candles everywhere. The old men's faces seem to have sprung from medieval paintings. Good wine.

I try to influence the Archbishop's Secretary against a formal commitment with Kerrl and give him specific advice on inviting the German churches to the Oxford conference. After dinner I explain my ideas about the European situation and English politics. The headmaster is practically the only one who has somewhat optimistic views—just as in Edinburgh. The faith of pedagogues! Late to bed.

May 5

Dr. Mannheim, a cousin of Karl's, takes me to Oxford Circus where I meet Anita and Margy. Many vain attemps to buy a suit. At last: success—it is dark gray with light gray stripes, costs £7.10s—$37.00. I also buy a raincoat.

Lunch at Margy's with Lothar but without Anita. Lothar is general· representative for the *Frankfurter Zeitung* in England—a steppingstone toward better things. He is very hostile to the Nazi regime but loves Germany; in his opinion, only a war will rid Germany of the Nazis. He also believes that war is inevitable.

Back to my hotel to pack; Loewe arrives for a discussion with Pollock.

May 6—Cambridge

I arise to warm sunshine, surrounded by fantastic birdsong. Long walk through most of the colleges and their gardens.

The most beautiful sight is the King's College Chapel, built by Henry VIII; it has huge old glass windows and a most exquisitely fashioned Gothic ceiling. Behind the main colleges there is the river with bridges, meadows, rowboats. Photographs. It is very warm. A visit to Fitzwilliam Museum.

Back to my quarters where the Dean of Caius College (pronounced Keess College) calls for me. Lunch with self-service. We walk to one of the houses by way of the well-built new library. Then by car over green hills, from where we have a wide view, as in a Dutch landscape.

To my quarters; then, with my briefcase, to the riverbank. Coffee at Lyons. Students in fencing masks fence outdoors by the river. There are tennis courts nearby and boats on the water.

There is a comparatively small audience for my lecture, which is well received. Kantorowitz is present. I discuss the situation of the Church with Canon Raven and Principal Gibbon, both members of the Committee for Foreign Affairs of the Church of England. Someone reports on a decision against the Kerrl committees.

Dinner at the college, where sherry and cider are served in ancient silver mugs. Coffee is taken in a little separate garden full of flowering trees.

Dr. Sommel calls for me. Before we leave, Raven thanks me for my lecture. As the first foreign lecturer, I have helped him in his efforts to counteract the insularity of English theology.

Sommel is Lecturer in German at Cambridge. As we walk, he tells fascinating stories about his trip to Germany while the elections were going on. He estimates that 60% voted for Hitler. He believes that without the Rhineland, it would have been 40%. He maintains that the Rhinelanders themselves wanted the French to march in and would have killed the Nazis. All the older groups are still there, he says, they are not organized, but are waiting for "the event." At the universities: total despair.

Around nine o'clock I call for Kantorowitz at the Caius College "combination room," and we go to his apartment where we share a bottle of Moselle. We are in complete agreement on English politics and on what our task in England must be. Later his wife joins us. She is very nice and lively. We talk about Hilde-Dore and the Bachmann group's attitude toward her; about his dealings with the New School, and about how happy he is at Cambridge. Both walk back with me, through meadows and fields, under a full moon.

May 7

I have had them wake me at seven o'clock. It is a foggy morning. I pack and return to London where Loewe meets me at the station. My busy morning includes the purchase of a hat and a suitcase with the help of Julia Mannheim. In the street I run into Professor I.P. Meyer from Berlin, whom I don't recognize at first. He tells me about Poelchau, Rathmann, Haubach, etc. He himself has had his house searched repeatedly, now wants to start a secondhand bookstore in London. He tells me about Fuchs, whose daughter-in-law gave birth to his grandchild in prison while her husband had to flee Germany.

I pack before lunch and, after lunch, leave for Birmingham where I am received by Mr. Wood. He is a Quaker, the leader of the Woodbrokers and a member of Oldham's philosophy of history section. We have tea in one of the houses, accompanied by a heated discussion of English politics and of power in general. The garden is beautiful and full of birds. We walk across some meadows and past the little rill called Woodbrook to the main house which is an excellent example of Baroque architecture. I am given the same room in which Rabindranath Tagore and Gandhi had slept.

Enter Heinrich Becker, Quaker, one-time official at the Kultusministerium under Grimme. Also: Baumgart, formerly Privatdozent in Berlin—a friend of Christian Hermann—

with his wife; Dr. Rotholz, a friend of the photographer Stephi Brandl. He carries a large photograph of me with him, for advertising purposes. At the students' tables, girls—from every country in the world—are in the overwhelming majority.

After dinner I lecture on the idea and the future of Religious Socialism, which creates a strong impression. Short discussion period follows. The Germans say that my lecture gave them "feelings of home." A smaller discussion group contains Communist students. They explain, in the interest of dialectic materialism, that religion says "God is," and Communism says "God is not," which they say is not a dialectical relation but a contradiction.

After the discussion I go to visit Baumgart. We talk in German and drink orange juice. One feels closer to Germany here. There is a greater urgency toward change, and less resignation than in America.

I sleep well in Gandhi's bed.

May 8

Heinrich Becker brings me breakfast. We continue our talk in the garden, beside the pond.

We drive to Wesley College, which is also the theological faculty of Birmingham University. I give a fifty-five-minute lecture on "The Religious Interpretation of History." The students are alert and react strongly.

I hurry to the station—accompanied by Mr. Taillor who belonged to the Frankfurt Seminar and is now Assistant here —to catch the train to Oxford. Arrive in Oxford too early, and take a car to the apartment of Dr. Crossmann who is a Fellow at New College. The apartment is located in a re-modeled stable that was built six hundred years ago. The view from the window is one of the courtyard, a garden, and some chickens. Crossmann, who was in my course at Frank-furt, speaks perfect German.

Having unpacked, I take a short walk through the college, with its ancient stone wall, its beautiful garden, church, and cloister. And then, immediately, another walk with Crossmann who is only twenty-eight, very cheerful and not at all shy. We climb up into the old tower of New College from where we have a panoramic view of the Middle Ages and, farther away, the suburbs with their residential and industrial sections.

Tea with Crossmann and Kloepper (a young lawyer, immigrant). After this I lecture to about fifty people at Manchester College. Among the listeners are Teddy and Burchard. Afterward we say hello to each other and arrange for a meeting later on.

I dress and go to dinner and Mansfield College. In the Principal's apartment there are about fourteen professors. I present my views on the general situation. There follow discussions of theology and of the political situation; later the talk centers on the historical Jesus.

By car to Teddy's apartment. Indescribably good wine. And human, heart-to-heart talk. Teddy wants to have Hannah's poems as quickly as possible. His address is: Merton College—the oldest, most unbelievably beautiful of the colleges.

Late to bed.

May 9

Crossmann takes a bath while I shave. Teddy calls for me and we walk through the main colleges. There is a wealth of beauty wherever you look—the buildings, the gardens—all are beautiful. The Cathedral has round columns and a window depicting Thomas à Becket. Beautiful Christ Church Quadrangle.

Lunch at Crossmann's with Teddy. Then Mrs. Baker takes us in her car to the park of the Duke of Marlborough. The park is pure Gainsborough, a picture of incredible charm, come to life. The most fantastic trees, water with a stone bridge across it, the palace; everything is steeped in the most delicate haze.

Later, a long walk through a huge private estate; countless flowers, orchids, rabbits, birds; the entire atmosphere is green and hazy.

To tea at the Burchards', where I find Mr. and Mrs. Olden, Teddy, and Hermann Usener. At first Olden and I talk about his and Heiden's Hitler books. That same evening he sends me his book. He wants to do the paper on the Republic; I describe my plan for getting all participants to work together. There follows a difficult discussion of the *Frankfurter Zeitung*. Teddy is very abstract and doctrinaire. All the rest are in favor of the paper and consider it a means of strengthening the critical spirit inside the country.

To New College. I change and proceed to the high-table, where I share a bottle of Rhine wine with Crossmann. Next to me is Foster, a Fellow at Christ Church, who once studied under Kroner and me in Dresden.

We carry our table napkins to the round table where port and coffee are served. According to ancient tradition, the wines are handed around three times before coffee is served. Past the fireplace on a special walk. Then up to Crossmann's room under the eaves. Discussion about the variability of categories. At 10:30 Hermann drops in and joins in our discussion. At 11:00 we all go to Teddy's music friends, where he plays in a quintet. They play Beethoven. The host's wife is American, very charming; she is the daughter of old Taussig, whom I had met at Harvard, through Ulich. My first experience of American patriotism. Nocturnal walk with Crossmann through the dream garden of New College.

May 10

At breakfast I have a talk about Christianity and politics with Dr. Mand who has come especially to see me. Then I call for Hermann at Burchard's, and we walk through the gardens of Magdalen College. Unimaginably beautiful. We talk at length about his attitude which is factually quite unequivocal but tactically very difficult; about the possibility of his emigrating; about his breakdown after the move to Munich; about currents in art-historical research, etc. At first he is terribly excited, later on very sweet.

We have lunch at Burchard's, where we also meet Teddy. After lunch I have a long talk with Burchard.

Teddy and Hermann take me to the train after I have said good-by to Crossmann and New College.

I arrive in London, at Paddington Station, exactly as I did on my first day on English soil. By car to the Mannheims', where I get into a big and very important discussion with them and Loewe, which continues until 2:00 A.M.

May 11

To the Red Court Hotel where I meet Mrs. Mellinger who has news about the Spiegelbergs. She herself wants to marry Metmann. She is Jewish and they both had to leave. She is a very fine person, a member of Jung's Eranos circle in Zurich. She tells me that Metmann was run over by a car, and lost both legs. Also, that Wagner was dismissed after his house had been searched. An SS man had denounced him, as a result of a rather tame show of his paintings in Berlin.

Rade is in Berlin and lives on a small pension. Elis lives in Berlin and wants to marry the silversmith, Rosenberg. Friedrich has matured a great deal, which also shows in his seminar. Roesli is a little devil; she keeps Friedrich from spending more time with his children who have been farmed out to both sets of grandparents.

Lunch at the Earl of Listowel's—I am alone with the Earl and his wife. I report on my travels and impressions and on the political situation. I reject the two-worlds theory in religion. The Earl's wife asks about the situation of the

Catholic Church and declares herself glad that, as a Catholic, she is exempt from such philosophical problems.

I meet Ursula Niebuhr at the French Line office and take her to the train for Oxford. Before boarding it, she says: "Now we'll do it the European way," and lets me kiss her cheek, which I find extremely sweet of her.

Left alone, I stroll through Kensington Gardens and Hyde Park. On the park benches there are many cocottes. I admire the wonderful tulip beds and pass many deck chairs for hire.

I change my clothes for the Schairers' party. At the party I meet: Hans Simon, the Lothars, the Moholy-Nagys, Hergesell, two families I do not know, among them a nice Swiss woman, and the two girls from the German Embassy. I dance conscientiously with everyone, later take some people home. Then, when everyone has left, I attack Schairer in a way that completely overwhelms him: I demand a clear-cut affirmation of the immigrant situation. We must begin to feel at home in the New World without regard for what is going on back in Germany—and he agrees.

I have to sleep over at the Schairers' because the last train has long since gone. Just as the birds begin their morning concert, I fall asleep.

May 12

I wake up with a slight hangover due to one glass of whiskey. Mannheim and I call on Demuth and talk about the immigrant situation. About seven hundred have still not been placed.

Back to the Mannheims' for a change of clothes and lunch. After lunch I take a nap with a hot water bottle against my lumbago. Then I pack on a grand scale, make some last telephone calls, have supper. And then I am off to Liverpool Street Station.

The train to Harwich goes through the East End of London. There is an evening mood over the landscape. I have become fond of England. But when Adolf and Karl asked me whether I would change places with them, my answer was more No than Yes. This impressed them deeply, as far as America is concerned.

We approach Harwich where the night boat to Holland awaits us. First passport inspection as we go on board. I have a pleasant cabin to myself. Briefly, I look out at the harbor, at the sea. Soon afterward I fall asleep.

May 13

The steward wakes me at 5:15 with the famous English cup of tea. I am suffering from intense lumbago. The ship has arrived at Hoek and there is a second passport inspection; then we have to go through customs. Our train, with its German cars, passes the mythical "Rheingold" train, which turns out to be no better than an English train of third-class carriages. Everyone speaks German.

The train traverses a truly Dutch landscape, even flatter and richer in water and cattle than the English countryside. The first tulip beds, the first windmill, come into sight.

In Amersfoort, Leni Mennicke awaits me at the station. Karolus is away on a trip, but will be back tomorrow. After a short drive through pine woods, we arrive at the school. There are a main house, a lodge, the Mennickes' house. I have a room at the lodge, since Mennicke's house is too crowded—with two children, an assistant and a maid.

We walk through green shimmering birch woods and sunny meadows. There are soldiers stationed nearby. Behind a wire fence, under some pine trees, Karola plays with a huge dog. Ruth has become a pretty girl of fourteen. Fienchen, the Dutch maid, or rather, governess, eats with the family and speaks lovely Dutch. The assistant, Heinz, is planning to become a teacher. After lunch I sleep a little, then we take a wonderful bicycle ride across the heath and into town. We inspect an ancient tower and the moat, then stop for Bols at a real inn. The bicycle ride seems to have massaged away my lumbago. After dinner I start sorting my letters. A huge mountain of mail has accumulated. At 8:30 we have tea— a Dutch tradition. Early to bed, after a starlit stroll under the trees.

May 14

This morning I feel tired, although I had plenty of sleep. In England I overexerted myself, and this is beginning to tell on me now.

I take a beautiful walk among some good-sized estates, then sleep for an hour before lunch. After lunch I ride a bicycle through several villages.

Karolus and von de Waters arrive. They have traveled by car through Belgium and the Ardennes.

We have tea under the pines, but a thunderstorm drives us inside. On my first morning here I had a letter from Hannah, acknowledging her receipt of my day-to-day reports. After the rainstorm the birches give off the same fragrance as those birches in the Vogelstrasse did: bitter and young.

Karolus plays with Karola while I write some letters. The airplanes overhead, the soldiers nearby, the low-slung pines— it all reminds me of those army camps in the Champagne during the war.

After dinner we stroll along the birch path. Teatime is at 8:30. I get into the first important conversation with Karolus —over a bottle of wine. Our basic political attitudes are more compatible than they used to be. His position here seems secure; he will get a kind of foundation professorship in Amsterdam, but will continue to live in Amersfoort. He admits that social pedagogy is necessary—not in Holland, but in America; which is exactly what Mannheim and Loewe have said.

May 15

Summertime begins in Holland and we lose another hour. I sit in a deck chair in the boiling sun, preparing my lecture. A young writer comes and brings Karolus a book: *Ave Caesar*. He stays for lunch, and afterward he and I have a long talk about the psychology of Holland's young people. His views are similar to Schairer's: disintegration, visions of war and death. As an example, he describes a recent art exhibit which showed a marked emphasis on death. He is very much impressed by the program idea.

Karolus and I drive to Amsterdam through flowering meadows and between many canals. We call on Dr. Ide, who lives at Brueghelstrass No. 10. The house is quite modern and has good lines. The Ides occupy the ground floor and the first floor. The Landauers, from Frankfurt, live above them and have their own separate entrance.

We take liqueur with Bols in the little garden. Dr. Ide has a strong, wide, physician's face. His wife is small and lively and wears glasses. Dinner guests arrive who have been invited to hear my lecture. I see many good faces. My lecture is to be a kind of chat about Europe and America. I present my impressions of the various towns and landscapes; I talk about art, economy, education, and the churches, relating it all to the contrast between the tragic and the ethical situation. Questions and a discussion follow. My talk seems to have aroused quite a lot of interest. The Sinzheimers are present, too. Later, after the party has dwindled down to a small group, the talk continues for a long time. Karolus has to go back to Amersfoort, but I am staying at the Ides' in a beautiful large room. There is a lot of good wine.

May 16

Mrs. Ide drives me into town where I buy a necktie to go with my new English suit. Before that, I have coffee with

Dr. Ide at eleven o'clock, between breakfast and lunch—another Dutch custom.

We look into some antique shops with paintings, then visit the university. Everything is incredibly beautiful.

After lunch Mrs. Ide leaves for Amersfoort and I go to the Sinzheimers' house to prepare for my evening lecture. Suddenly, my English teacher from Frankfurt—Miss Menschke—turns up. At first I don't recognize her and don't even remember her name. Then we make an appointment to go to the seashore together this coming Sunday.

At four o'clock E. visits me. She is very happy with her friend, though she cannot marry him; and she is successful in her profession. Her friend is a small, sturdy "100% Aryan," a designer of stage settings and advertisements.

At 6:30, dinner at the Landauers'. They are a charming family, with sweet, happy children. He has a flourishing practice and is highly respected here.

There is a small group in the lecture hall. I speak on "Anthropology and the Philosophy of Religion." As I enter the hall. I meet Geza Berger and Miss Nussbaum (from the philosophy seminary in Frankfurt). An interesting debate about ways of interpreting theological symbols follows my lecture. In the back of the hall I have noticed a lady whom I recognize later, after my lecture: she is Ina Rudolph, now married to an art historian named Trivas. She seems quite "settled." Geza, on the other hand, looks dried up and aged. We all meet again at the Landauers'. Miss Rudolph tells me about her experience with Fritz Opel. We agree to meet once more next week.

The Ides and I sit up later over a bottle of wine. I am overcome with psychoanalytical feelings.

May 17

Today is Hannah's birthday, and a magnificent morning. I meet Miss Menschke at the railroad station and we take the train to Zaandfoot. Next to the railroad tracks, countless bicyclists are on the road, making an almost medieval picture. We pass the Dome of Haarlem. The beach is vast and dotted with wicker beach chairs. We lie in the hot sun amidst the Amsterdam Sunday crowds.

Miss Menschke, lively and nice, had quietly sneaked out of Germany. Her friend is Jewish, etc. She is completely out of touch with Menzels. We watch the bathers in the sun and in the water. At noon, after Miss Menschke has left, I take a beach chair and write a letter to Hannah who must be just getting up at this time.

There is music and girls are dancing as in a van Steen painting. Sailboats; and, in the distance, an ocean liner, perhaps bound for America.

Back to Amsterdam to the Dutch psychoanalyst v. d. Hoop and his beautiful wife, an Austrian Baroness. We dine together at the Lido Restaurant, surrounded by water and trees. The food is very good. True to Dutch custom, they congratulate me on Hannah's birthday. v. d. Hoop has shifted from Jung to Freud. His wife knows everyone in Frankfurt society. She has spent much time in Frankfurt and liked it there. Now, she says, it has become a wasteland. They invite me to their house.

At nine o'clock to the Sinzheimers', who are preparing for their daughter's wedding. Both seem somewhat depressed by their expatriation. He has plenty of opportunity to work, but not many students. She has not quite settled in yet, misses many things, but is very sweet; she remembers our costume party with great enthusiasm, says it was the best party of her life. We drink to Hannah's health. I talk with Sinzheimer about the "program" and the "History of the Republic." His own plan is quite similar to ours, but he has a publisher. All that's missing is money for the employees' wages. I will try to effect a merger of the two plans.

May 18

I get up late, write some letters, pack, visit the Rijksmuseum. "The Night Watch," "The Steelmeesters," "The Jewish Bride." To look at anything more will simply be too much. Even Vermeer is crushed by Rembrandt's overpowering greatness. There is always just one really great man who makes us aware of man's true potential.

Back to Amersfoort without lunch. Fields of flowering Scotch broom glow in the sun. Chestnut trees; lilac bushes. I prepare my lecture for Utrecht.

Karolus and I ride to the railroad station on bicycles, then continue to Utrecht by train. The train follows the bank of the Single amid blossoming trees. We have dinner at Professor Franken's. My lecture, which I give at the Geographic Institute, is on "Existential Philosophy and Pragmatism." Dr. Kraft from Frankfurt is among the listeners. Afterward there is a good discussion with good people. The main problem: Logos and Existence. Karolus and I stop for beer with Franken and Kraft before returning to Amersfoort. We ride our bicycles home through the night.

May 19

I wake up with a hangover headache. During a short walk with Leni I see a great many soldiers. Later I work sitting in the sun under rustling pines.

Karolus and Leni take me to Amsterdam from where I continue on to Leyden, alone. The train passes late-blooming tulip fields, incredibly brilliant in color. Two students wait for me at the station and take me sightseeing through the cathedral and the town. The cathedral is large and cold, devastated by Protestantism. At the moment, the plaster is being removed from the wonderful brickwork it had covered. Proletarian streets along some of the canals. Photographs. Old Peoples' homes. Old Father Rhine.

There is vermouth before dinner with the students who are very nice. Then I speak at the old university about the "Un-tragic Consciousness in America, and the Tragic Consciousness in Europe." A heated discussion follows. The New Testament scholar, de Swan, attacks me for being non-Dutch. But scarcely anyone comes up with a factual objection. The students do not take part in the debate. Afterward they say that it was an interesting evening because of the clash of ideas.

Back to Amsterdam, where Karolus and Leni call for me and take me back to Amersfoort.

May 20

Friday; it is sunny and windy. I go for a stroll with Mrs. Ide, Karolus' sponsor, who is very fond of him. He still is overworked, but she tells me that he will get an "endowed chair" at the University of Amsterdam in the fall. She has worked very hard to raise the funds for it. Karolus is still quite depressed and somewhat irritable. After lunch I go to town with Ruth and buy her a bathing suit which looks very nice on her. She is delighted. Afterward, a long bicycle ride with Leni. Among other places, we visit an old park which belongs to a palace. I am becoming more and more enchanted by the Dutch landscape. The Dutch themselves seem a thickheaded lot who have not yet quite found out what is going on in the world. After dinner I call for Lilly Pincus in Amersfoort. She has not changed much, but is exhausted by the last few weeks.

In the evening, at Karolus', we have our first serious discussion in Mrs. Ide's presence. I explain my ideas and plans. Karolus is quite negative, partly for personal reasons, partly because of his situation in Holland. I struggle desperately but in vain. Lilly's criticism seems to have a Communist viewpoint (later I find out that this is indeed the case). I go to bed very depressed.

71

May 21

At eight o'clock everyone is awakened by Mr. Ide who has come from Amsterdam in his car. It is Ascension Day. Mr. and Mrs. Ide, Lilly and I travel by car across Holland. We visit a palace which dates back to about 1550 and is now owned by an advertising man whom the Ides know. Breakfast at the hotel, overlooking the Rhine and a vast landscape. An old palace on the water looks very picturesque. We stop for lunch atop a mountain from where we can see all the way to Germany. I see it without any feeling of homesickness. Dead, destroyed; barbed wire and Gestapo.

We continue through the lovely countryside to the house of a Socialist, a former high official in the Dutch East Indies, which are here simply called "India." After a walk through a landscape that reminds me of the Mark Brandenburg, we drive to the Zuider Sea. Through the old maritime city of Kampen with its many turrets, to the harbor. There is a violent northwester blowing, which produces flat, white-crested waves. The dam locks in the sea completely. We drive between endless meadows on top of a series of dams. On the way back to Amersfoort we stop for dinner at a restaurant. I bring back two smoked eels for Karolus who is delighted with them. Early to bed.

May 22

During a long walk, Lilly and I have our first talk; about Hirzel, Klaere, the Kuessel, Lilly's work. Hirzel has been dismissed; his magazine was not considered acceptable. He is quite primitive in political matters but has established himself in the Kuessel through his personal warmth and—occasional—personal courage. Schneider has turned up again, too. The whole thing is a purely personal matter. In actual practice, Lilly and Fritz are treated as possible enemies, which means that nobody tells them anything. Fritz is clear-sighted and determined; if he should be forced to leave, they will both go to Russia. They study Russian for hours every day. The trip to Palestine is for business only; they have not the slighest intention to emigrate. Lilly helps many people and is very active as an agitator. The other day M. answered a matrimonial ad and gave her age as less than it actually is. Whereupon she was promptly denounced and G. had to go to the police. It turned out that she had done this only because of the matrimonial ad. But G. was thoroughly frightened. The situation in Palestine is very bad. Claire had to stay in the hotel during their entire time in Jerusalem. They could visit the Dead Sea only under police escort.

I work my way through a mountain of official mail. Leave for Bentorf between Haarlem and Zaandfoort, to visit the Woodbrookers. De Voss calls for me and takes me straight to the dinner table. He had heard me speak in 1930.

A quiet hour in Banning's house. Karolus arrives with Mrs. Ide. I lecture on "Protestantism in the Present World Situation," after which there is a none-too-successful debate about Barth. I have a feeling that I can no longer give good lectures in German.

By car to Amsterdam. Karolus dances with Mrs. Ide. I merely look on, since I don't feel in the mood. Both of us spend the night at the Ides', after drinking some white Bordeaux.

May 23

Up late, I take the traditional eleven o'clock coffee with Mrs. Ide and Karolus at the Hotel Americain where I stayed in 1930.

From 12:30 to 1:30—A. and I talk about W.; she warns me about W.'s gossiping, and also about her social contact with young Nazis.

For lunch to the Reveszes'. He is pessimistic about Gelb (a few days ago I had a very nice and hopeful letter from

73

Nelly). Revesz feels very much a stranger in Holland. He criticizes Karolus for his tendency to turn into a Dutchman too quickly. He himself seems to be rather unpopular here. His wife, who writes books on art history, impresses me as an interesting and attractive person.

I see Miss Menschke briefly. She wants to go to South Africa or America.

I change into a dinner jacket at the Ides'. With Mrs. Ide to a performance at the Wagner-Verein: they are playing *A Midsummer Night's Dream*, with music by Mendelssohn, under the direction of Willem Mengelberg. Wonderful performance: *the* social event of Amsterdam. The Crown Princess arrives precisely on time and everyone rises to great her. Mengelberg gives her an ovation; we sing the national anthem. During the long intermission there is a gala reception in the foyer. Mrs. Ide knows everyone; the Chief Mayor of Amsterdam, the Socialist Mayor; the Minister of Culture; the Commanding General, the ballerina Georgi. Many old gentlemen with medals and long beards—as in the days of old. The whole thing is a little like a puppet show depicting a period in the past. The Princess (future Queen) is twenty-eight years old and unmarried. She is fat and blonde, but seems likable.

Afterward Mrs. Ide and I visit two restaurants: one bourgeois and one Bohemian place. Mixture of intellectuals, prostitutes, couples, and solid citizens looking on. Very European. Late to bed.

May 24

A rainy morning. Round trip through the canals with Mrs. Ide. The patrician Herrengracht; through locks into the harbor where many big ocean liners lie at anchor. We try to get back through the locks, but can't: all the locks are closed. So we climb out across a freight barge, right into the Jewish market, which is in full swing on this Sunday morning. Fas-

cinating types. Rembrandt's house; the old synagogues.

Lunch at the Ides', a nap, packing. By car to Amersfoort with Mrs. Ide and son. Wonderful drive along the canals and old villas. The landscape is incomparably beautiful. All the meadows are in bloom, and so are the chestnut trees, lilac bushes, and laburnum. Immense horizon; countless cattle. We stop at the most beautiful old seaside palace, now owned by an art dealer who has put all kinds of good things on display inside. We meet Revesz and his wife, with two professors. In the palace yard, coffee and cake—as in Treptow.

Arrival in Amersfoort. The Ides leave and Karolus, Lilly, and I visit the fabulously situated Berghotel to make inquiries on behalf of Hannah's parents who have announced that they are coming.

Back through Scotch broom and young birches. A long talk with Karolus at last shows some fruitful results. His hostile rigidity is beginning to dissolve.

Late to bed.

May 25

A wonderful morning. I write some letters, outdoors, until noon. Then I walk with Leni who always gives an impression of being overburdened.

Off to the Hague where the chairman of the Philosophical Society calls for me. I am to stay at the house of Pastor Fetter, who is trying to combine psychoanalysis with the ministry.

I lecture at the Society, to twenty-five first-rate men from various academic and artistic professions. Tremendous success, brilliant debate. Some blame the basic disagreement I encountered in Leyden on the state of liberal theology there. I am asked about the possibility of this kind of realism, seen from the theological viewpoint.

Seated at the director's table, I meet a painter who was once a member of the Church in Dresden (Fritz Bienert) and knew us all. After the debate we spend a little time in a restaurant, over wine and mayonnaise (very European). Then Fetter and I go home to his apartment.

May 26

Breakfast with Fetter and his very nice, incredibly well-read wife—I feel like a barbarian because I never read.

With my suitcase to the railroad station. I meet Mrs. Duthil, formerly Mrs. van Hall, from Rotterdam (she was in Frankfurt once; in 1930, she drove me to the Zuider Sea).

The Mauritz Huis is not as overwhelming as I remembered it. Vermeer's *View of Delft*, and Rembrandt's *Saul and David*. Mrs. Duthil (bank directress) asks many expert questions. I take her to her stepdaughter's, then go to buy my ticket for Paris.

A visit to the Prisoners'-Poort, a trip to Haarlem (where I find the Hals Museum closed), the cathedral, the meat market, and through little streets. Back in Amsterdam, I have coffee in a restaurant on the bank of the canal, while writing this.

Dinner at the Ides' with Karolus. Very cheerful. Karolus leaves with Mrs. Ide. I have a visit from Mrs. Trivas. She tells me that since her release from political imprisonment she has tried to become an actress; happened to meet Fritz v. Opel; had some success on the stage, went on tour with Moissi; tried to get an engagement somewhere in the provinces; someone denounced her in connection with her past; result: no provincial engagement. Fight with Opel, difficult life in Berlin where she worked as a typist without knowing how to type. Six years ago she met the Russian emigree, Trivas; married him last year. They are now living in Amsterdam. He is quite good-looking, with beautiful eyes. She says she was ashamed to come back.

An hour later Mrs. Ide knocks on the door, calling out that it is time to start our evening on the town as planned. We dispose of Mrs. Trivas. But fate catches up with me at the very first place we enter—in the form of a Mr. and Mrs. Y. who had heard my lecture. She is very pretty, acquainted with Ide who successfully tries to dispel her Nazi ideas. We go into a bar, the two men sit down at a bar table, and I try to continue working on the lady. Her Nazi sympathy is based on vague feelings of belonging and community. We go to the Y.'s for a short visit, and sit around their lovely fire; then, home.

May 27

I get up late and pack, then off to Amersfoort to call for Hannah's parents. As I write this, I am sitting under an elm at the station, waiting for the train.

Hannah's parents have arrived; old, sweet, pale. The trip was a very exciting experience for them. Now they stand on the platform, twelve guilders in their pockets, and are visibly relieved because I am here. I take them into the car and up the "mountain" where the Berghotel stands on one of the most beautiful spots in Holland, with a panoramic view over plains and forests. They are given a good room, and we have lunch together. They are glad to be out; they feel psychologically under pressure, spiritually cut off. Father grumbles so audibly that I have to stop him for fear of possible spies. Both are delighted about René. I show them the photos that arrived yesterday. At the sight of Erdmuthe's picture, Mother Werner thinks at first that it is a picture of Hannah as a little girl. They want to stay till after Pentecost. We drink a bottle of wine to Hannah's health. After lunch I go back to the camp, sleep, take a walk, dine with Karolus and the whole family plus Lilly and the assistant; then Leni and I go on bicycles to visit the Werners, find them in a back room, drinking tea. We take a wonderful walk through birches, spruce, and broom, with nightingales singing all around us; Leni walks with Mother, I with Father. He tells me how well all the children are doing. Only Roland has been dismissed and wants to join the army; we hope he will get in. Back home. Talk with Karolus, close, human. Then to bed and boundless sleep.

May 28

Cool and windy; a brisk walk with Lilly who had gone to Amsterdam alone. She tells me very interesting details about the Russian lessons she and Fritz are taking together, secretly, from an enthusiastic Russian who is officially allowed to teach Hebrew only. She is also learning something about the dynamics of life in Russia today from him. They want to go there next year, but this, again, can only be done with a special passport which they have to get in Prague.

In my room, the peonies spread their fragrance and remind me of the feast of Pentecost which has fallen into oblivion in America (peonies are called "Pentecost Roses" in German).

I begin to worry about my series of lectures: four days in a row, morning and afternoon. (I will write again on the morning of the last day of the course). Work and walks. In the afternoon at five, a drive to Hilversum with Hannah's parents and Lilly. Past villas and parks to the Hilversum Town Hall, perhaps the most beautiful modern building I know. Yellow brick with blue and white lines in between, very wide and varied in shape, surrounded by water and flowers. Inside, all modern furnishings. Unfortunately, we get thrown out quite soon: there are no more guided tours today.

A warming glass of brandy at the hotel. Back to the Amersfoort station to wait for M. L. General disappointment when she does not show up. I take Hannah's parents back to the hotel. Work; early to bed.

May 29

I walk, work, and cash travelers cheques. After lunch, on foot to Mrs. de Jongheer, the mother of Cola Heiden who is married to Margaret Stern's brother. Nice elderly Dutch woman who asks me a lot of searching questions about her children. She shows me her garden and the homemade pool, and is sad because her famous dog does not act as lively as he should.

A visit to the Werners', then work in the garden with a wonderful view. Dinner with Hannah's parents and Lilly. She is very good with Father, which leaves me free to talk to Mother. While Lilly takes the Werners down to the camp, I ride to the station and pick up M. L. who has arrived at last. She looks marvelous and is in a most effervescent mood.

At night there is a festive gathering at the Mennickes' in the Werners' honor. Karolus is charming, M. L. full of sparkle and talk, the Werners are happy, Leni is a delightful hostess. M. L. tells us, and proves by her own example, how well informed people are in Germany. She describes a kind of arithmetic book in which the schoolchildren get this type of problem: "One bomb kills twenty people; how many people can twenty bombs kill?" She says it is no longer possible to take an ironically superior attitude; one must reject the whole thing matter-of-factly, though carefully. Everyone is quite aware of the election swindle. She speaks very positively about Elisabeth and Erhardt.

Hannah's parents return to the hotel. The rest of us sit up until late into the night.

May 30

Final preparations for my lectures. M. L. is visiting her parents, brings them down to us at 3:30.

The course opens; there are approximately thirty people, students, elderly ladies, schoolteachers, also: Geza Berger, Miss Menschke, Miss Nussbaum from the philosophical seminar, and a nice family of Communist emigrants; Mr. v. Mandele, in whose house in Rotterdam I spoke in 1930; Mrs. Ide, M. L.—Karolus gives the opening address in which he welcomes Hannah's parents. I speak before and after dinner on "The Crisis of the Liberal State in All Countries of the World." The discussion is to the point, but still feeble. Later, wine at Karolus', then work in bed till two.

May 31

Up at six and work until eight-thirty. Mrs. Ide brings me breakfast so I can have a little more time. At ten o'clock I lecture on "The Idea, Types and Movements of the Spirit." Evidently, my lecture makes a strong impression. In the afternoon, from three to five: discussion.

M. L. goes to visit her parents. We spend an informal evening, and Tolstoi's story about *The Three Hermits and the Bishop* is read aloud. I talk with the architect, Mrs. Falkenberg, about Russian architecture.

In between I continue to prepare for my next lecture. Very strenuous; thoughts keep going through my head all night.

A glass of beer with Karolus, then to bed, where I continue my preparation.

June 1

At ten o'clock I lecture on "The People and The State," pinpointing the German ideology. After lunch, discussion of the economic situation.

Preparation for the evening lecture, the last of the series. The Werners stay in the hotel: Mother has caught a cold. The weather is icy. My final lecture offers the solution inherent in the idea of the religious-socialist alliance. Afterward everyone gathers around the fireplace and I have to talk about America. Dead tired to bed.

June 2

Ten o'clock, final discussion, outdoors, in the warm sunshine. The Werners come, too. Speeches expressing gratitude; speeches of farewell. The course was a great success, the discussion had been at a consistently high level, the whole thing was very well managed by Leni and Karolus. After the farewell luncheon, to bed where I write a birthday letter to my father. He has offered to give Elisabeth 200 marks for the journey, but he himself does not want to come.

By car through the beautiful Dutch countryside with the Werners and M. L. We visit an ancient village on the Zuider Sea. Everyone there is in native costume; the children especially are cute. Very old narrow streets with low-slung houses, like dollhouses, and crowds of people in native dress. Beautiful fishing port. We drive back over the dykes to pay another visit to the Hilversum Town Hall.

I say good-by to the Werners at their hotel. Both are deeply moved. Mother wants to get the inheritance free by making it over to René. The question is whether it can be done. Both were very sweet, Mother very gray. On their way back they are going to visit some relatives at The Hague.

Dinner at the Mennickes' with our beloved M. L. Then I take her to the train. She talks about the collapse of ideals and how impossible it is to go on fighting the thing with irony. She insists that the Psychoanalytical Society has not been dissolved, but admits that it is struggling desperately. We had a very charming evening with her. She longs for letters from Hannah.

In the evening Karolus and I discuss our respective positions. Result: his is progressive-optimistic, while mine is tragic-dialectic; his Erasmic—mine Lutheran. He rejects the idea of the daemonic and of catastrophe, which explains his completely negative stand on Communism. I am glad that the perpetual, palpable tension between us has at last been given clear, conceptual expression.

June 3

I get up early to pack. Then I say good-by to Karolus and Karola. All leave-takings are different nowadays. One never knows when . . .

To the train with Leni and Lilly. I am going to Eushede at the German border to meet Staehlin. Lilly takes the same train all the way to Berlin. Communism and the things that have happened to her have turned her into a mature human being. Her infantile traits have disappeared. She tells me that for a year and half Fritz was facing the threat of imprisonment every day. They used to say good-by every morning as if it were forever. In their house, a woman, whose husband is in prison, gave birth to a child—that sort of thing is now happening all the time.

During my lectures Lilly made friends with the Communist couple. The man was so deeply stirred after my final lecture that he came the next day, all the way from Amsterdam, and asked me to turn my ideas into a pamphlet for clandestine distribution. I am writing this in a little waiting-room restaurant, waiting for Staehlin to arrive.

Finally he arrives, and we talk for four hours. It is one of my most important encounters on this entire journey. We start immediately, with the problem closest to his heart: the Confessing Church. His report is shattering: the most rigid, fanatical orthodoxy; anyone who disagrees on questions of dogma is instantly expelled. Denunciations are the order of the day. Everyone is required to submit unconditionally to the brotherhood counsels. A few weeks ago fourteen students boycotted his seminar because he was conducting exams together with "German Christians." Anyone who dares disagree is accused of heresy. On the other side, the Church committees are slowly but steadily working toward some kind of cooperation, for instance in Saxony. However, they may fail in the attempt, and if they do, there will be nothing left but the orthodox sect, fruit of Barthian theology.

Staehlin judges the world situation of Protestantism exactly as I do, which is to say: negatively. He sees it defenseless against Catholicism. At this point I read him the last paragraph of my "Protestantism in the Present World Situation," and he takes it down in shorthand. Amazing how much we still think alike after four years of separation! The idea of the religious order lies at the center of his thinking. He expresses his own conviction—shared by Oldham, he maintains—that all really decisive matters cannot really take effect for at least fifty years. He feels we must arm ourselves against the time of chaos. He himself has asked to be retired; he wants to become the Abbot of a Protestant monastery he founded near Rothenburg, Fulda. If the Kultusministerium refuses to pension him, he plans simply to quit. When he told this to his Dean, the Dean said, after a moment of shocked silence: "You still have a future. What you propose here is senseless."

Staehlin says that work at the universities is hopeless, work at the theological faculties senseless. Men from secular life—not young theology students—should be the leaders of the communities. He rejects Nazism unconditionally. He thinks that those who have gone through it might develop a new pagan Christianity which might be able to overcome the confessional split. He tells me that the leading Catholic liturgist, a Benedictine monk, said to him that they and his (Staehlin's) wing of the Protestant Church would someday fight side by side against Rome. But on the whole he is very pessimistic about the possibility of realizing his ideas in Germany. What he would like best would be to establish a German branch of the Anglican Church.

The Berneuchner Brotherhood has about 300 members. Each is assigned as a helper to another man. Staehlin, for instance, has been assigned to Frede, about whom he worries. He feels that Frede has never got over Johanna's death, and that he is thus unable to regain a fully positive orientation toward life. This, he says, makes him liturgically useless, nor can he give Trudchen a completely positive attitude toward life, or a feeling of fulfillment. Trudchen herself thinks that she won't live much longer. Staehlin also says that Ritter has developed very well, and was twice in prison . . . . He is suspicious of H.

Staehlin talks of daemonic sacraments and analyzes the Nazi swastika as a cross with claws instead of tails such as the real Indian sun-wheel has. He is reading Goethe's *Chromatology* in order to analyze the color *brown* (the color of the Nazis). He says he rarely has visions but is now plagued by one that shows Germany turned into a battlefield. On the day of Potsdam he cried all afternoon.

I broach the social angle. He admits that this is his weak point, but insists that the brotherhood's apolitical attitude and community organization must be regarded as symbolic. He does admit that such an attitude may bring with it the danger of seeming to support those in power. There is a contradiction here concerning their basic intentions.

He speaks of S. and says he can no longer put down roots anywhere, that he has taken to the nomadic life: the breaking of his engagement is a typical example. It is, Staehlin says, too late for him.

The total impression of our meeting: the idea of the religious order is encountered everywhere. Nobody believes any longer that the masses can be directly reeducated. This is a retreat, to be sure. But it also makes it possible for the leading intellectual and religious forces to regroup and gather strength.

At eight o'clock we say good-by, our friendship reaffirmed.

Past Amersfoort to Amsterdam. Magnificent sunset. Beautiful entrance into Amsterdam past the illuminated harbor. By car to the Ides' where, after a glass of wine, I go to bed, very tired.

June 4

I get up late, visit the de Hoops. He stays only for a little while, but we manage to have a pleasant conversation about Austria and Holland. An Austrian countess arrives and immediately spreads a delightful atmosphere of Old Vienna. Both she and Mrs. de Hoop are monarchists, and anti-Nazis.

85

The two ladies consider Starhemberg a "dashing" figure.

Lunch at the Sinzheimers'; we discuss the problem of the books. Then I go to say good-bye to the Ides, who are leaving for England. Ten minutes later I myself am at the railroad station.

To Brussels in a beautiful second-class carriage (which has been donated by the French Line). The border inspection is quick and easy.

Gaby's butler comes up to me, then Gaby herself appears, warm and cheerful as always, her face a vivid red. By car to 21 Avenue Victoria, at the edge of the Bois, which has the most wonderful trees. The house reminds me of Frankfurt, only a little smaller. The old familiar furniture and pictures are here. A very well-kept garden, many terraces. My room overlooks the Bois.

Dinner, with a torrent of questions and answers. Paul is very nice, the two boys have grown enormously and are intelligent. Gaby has become a little heavier in the face, but Paul is quite unchanged. He is working on problems of logic and managing his estate. We immediately get into a discussion.

To bed very early, with a good French book.

June 5

To town with Gaby. La Grande Place is the most beautiful square in the world—after San Marco. I admire the magnificent architecture of St. Gudule and regret the absence of good stained-glass windows. We wander through the harmoniously designed Street of Secretariats, past the Royal Palace, to the most beautiful house in Brussels, which is owned by Gaby's brother. Louis XVI outside and inside—full of beautiful things.

Mme. Evero receives us and regales us with wine. Later Paul comes to call for us there. But first Gaby and I look over the house. The most remarkable feature are two facing alcove beds in the upstairs bedroom: behind each bed is a mirror—which gives rise to certain jocular remarks, especially as the house was once owned by monks. There are several secret staircases, too.

Lunch at the Oppenheims' with invited guests. A professor of Byzantinism expresses—with brilliant French rhetoric —the very same views I had expounded in England. He says: the dictatorial countries are making history, and the democratic countries are making diplomacy. Next to me, a beautiful Australian woman wants to stab me with her table knife when I say she looks like an American. She hates all things colonial, as a result of her Australian experience. She says that Australia is like a nightmare for her.

Later I walk through the Bois with Paul, in the rain. We have coffee on the island. Magnificent trees everywhere. We argue about positivistic logic and come closer to each other's viewpoint than Paul ever did with Horkheimer, even though Horkheimer *is* a positivist.

At night Gaby and I go on the town. After a delightful dinner we visit a dance hall which is quite empty but pervaded by good atmosphere. Gaby shows me how to hold myself while dancing. On to a Russian place with intellectuals and, by American standards, an impossibly inept floor show. We try to speak French, but it is too strenuous for me in the long run. So we stick to English.

June 6

To the art gallery, by myself. It is wonderful, much more impressive than Rotterdam; the early Flemish school; Rogier van der Weyden; Hugo van der Goes; Gerard David; Petrus Christus; Patinir. A roomful of Cranach, another with small paintings by Rubens; a room of Brueghel and Bosch: *Bethlehem, The Fall of Icarus*, etc.

After lunch I change and go to a café. There I sit until about 5:30, writing and watching the stream of passers-by—

as in the old days. The people are a little too provincial.

At six o'clock there is a big cocktail party at the Oppenheims'. Eighty guests, beautiful women and clever men; a brilliant gathering of the *haute bourgeoisie* and intelligentsia of Brussels. Gaby's brother with his wife; a lovely Australian; a Swiss correspondent of the *Neue Zuericher Zeitung* to whom I explain my ideas and who agrees wholeheartedly. A Flemish Communist painter (female) with whom I discuss Diego Rivera; Dr. Hempel, Paul's co-worker in philosophy, with his beautiful wife. The party takes place indoors as well as out in the garden. There is dancing on the terrace. Though they are offering an abundance of cocktails, I have only one, knowing what they can do to you. My lack of French bothers me very much. I have to speak English all the time. French, which I used to love so, has become difficult, almost unpleasant for me.

Most of the guests leave at eight o'clock. At that time I walk to a nearby students' home, where N. is staying. She had written to Gaby and Gaby had got her a room there. N. has grown a little heavier, her eyes are greatly changed by her illness; but she is wide awake and full of life. She soon tells me that she had become converted to Catholicism last year. Now a member of the Catholic Caritas Society, she has to teach nuns in a big hospital in Cologne. She became a Catholic because she needed something beyond the finite, but she did not dare write about it because of the persecution of Catholics in Germany. After three quarters of an hour I have to return to the Oppenheims', to dress for a ball. I cannot accomplish this immediately because the remnants of the cocktail party—in highest spirits—have settled down all over the floor and are playing masquerade. The two Oppenheim sons, who are charming, surround the daughter of Vandevelde, a Bauhaus forerunner in Weimar. Only after an hour and a half of concerted effort, do Paul and Gaby manage to throw out the last of their guests. In other words, the party was a huge success.

Gaby and I change, and, with the lovely Australian leading the way, go to the ball which is being given at a club. A bit formal at first, then very gay—many beautiful women. I talk a great deal with an Austrian analyst who specializes in speech impediments. She is a little strange but very clever, acknowledges many mystical things, lectures on women's problems. Also, the lovely Australian, and a blonde with an interesting face and silver-tipped toes.

To bed around three.

June 7

René's birthday. There are moments when I have to suppress my longing for him with all my might. It is almost unbearable to think how he must be changing from day to day.

After a late breakfast, I go to see N. We have a very serious and good talk. She came to Catholicism on her own, without a father confessor; through reading and thinking. I challenge her by asking where she stands on the question of dogma, and find her completely unsure in this respect. First she tries to counter with the need for submission to dogmatic authority. Then she realizes that this is utterly impossible. She affirms the extrafinite aspect of the Church. She has many reasons for changing: a psychological reason, her loneliness after the coming of the Nazis; the impossibility of a concerted protest front, except within the framework of the Church; rejection of Protestantism, perhaps a form of protest against her father.

I explain my own position and it seems as if a new world were opening up for her. She is deeply grateful for the program idea and the idea of the religious order, regards it as a new way to approach the social question.

Lunch at the Oppenheims'. N. reports that anti-Catholic and especially antireligious-order laws are expected to be announced at the time of the Party Day. The prosecution of foreign-exchange smugglers and the League of Decency are the first steps in that direction.

She talks about Heidegger who, it appears, had been driven into the thing. She says that he now talks in such a dangerous way that one of his students had to come all the way from Berlin to warn him that he was in danger of being sent to a concentration camp. She says he is very upset, and that he now profoundly regrets the speech he made when he became rector. No one knows whether he will be able to recover. Riezler has been to see him again. And he has asked his former assistant Brock, whom he had treated so badly and who is now in England, to come back.

N. also tells us that last year the Catholics offered to enter into an alliance against the Nazis with the Evangelical Church, but the latter declined because of its own Nazi leanings.

N. and I spend an hour walking in the Bois which is heavy with rain and dark-moist; the birds sing like mad. Then I take her back to the students' home, and we say good-by.

The Oppenheims are enchanted with her. Dr. Hempel has come in the meantime, and we philosophize for three hours about truth and authenticity. But first I have to read Carnap. What is deeply shocking is the complete absence of any sphere of value. Value is regarded as a psychological factor. All very sterile. I retire to my room early, and am writing this, and am thinking of the birthday boy.

June 8

Up early. Gaby and I go to Ghent by train. Past wheat fields and tree-lined roads. It reminds me of the landscape in which the battle of the Somme was fought.

In Ghent, the cathedral and the Altar of Ghent (from which the stolen panel of the *Just Judges* is missing). Gaby is very good and thoughtful when looking at pictures. The donor portraits on the back of the panels are especially surprising.

We see: a magnificent municipal tower; a row of old guild houses along the waterfront; the castle of the Counts of Flanders, surrounded by water, thick-walled and uncanny inside. The City Hall is classical in style, built of corroded white-gray stone. Another half-hour's train ride takes us to Bruges. We have lunch in the wonderful marketplace where there is a whole string of restaurants, with tables extending deep into the square. French food, wine, medieval atmosphere. We walk through the ancient streets, along the canals with their tall trees and old stone bridges, to the cathedral. Then in a real horse-drawn carriage to the Beghinage which consists of many gray houses with green shutters. A large square with grass and trees lies at the center. Great silence. Farther on there is a nesting place for swans. The ground is white with feathers.

To the hospital where the Memling paintings are. They are much larger than I expected. But the very finest Memlings are at the museum, along with Weyden and van der Goes.

By boat through the canals. There is a different view every minute. On one of the bridges a girl sits reading, motionless, all afternoon. All of Bruges is like that.

After dinner de Man comes to visit. The Oppenheims welcome him briefly, then he and I talk from 8:30 to 11:30. This is a formidable task for him: only a few hours earlier his social-democratic party leader's attempt to form a cabinet ended in failure. He is very warm and friendly, and very grateful for Hannah's poems. He seems to have great influence with the cabinet, has himself been considered for the post of Prime Minister. Our discussion was in two parts: international politics and socialism, very rich and interesting. His political theory: Germany must be placated, i.e.: colonies, Austria, Eupen, Memel, the German part of Czechoslovakia, the Polish Corridor must be ceded to her. Those, he says, are legitimate claims. He further proposes: (1) A coalition between England, France, and Russia to force Hitler into serious negotiations, and (2) total disarmament of all

European countries, with an international control commission to be established in every country. He thinks it could be achieved but would be very difficult. But he sees no other road to peace, and he feels that to preserve the peace is the one absolutely necessary goal. In Belgium the fear of war is so great that Gaby is thinking of sending her boys to America. As for national politics, he is definitely critical of the workers' parties. He thinks that the times when they were the carriers of Socialism are over. He says he often feels helpless with disgust at his own party. He wants to build a kind of Socialism out of a combination of proletariat, Catholic Socialists, Flemish peasants, and the youth of Belgium. As this is exactly what Loewe and I had talked about, I tell him of the program-idea. He says that the practical work he is now doing makes him much happier than his theoretical work in Germany ever did. He would like to see an executive branch of the government established, independent of Parliament. We conclude our talk with the statement that Belgium is offering him a marvelous opportunity to experiment. For me, it all means a confirmation of my own thinking. If the war should devastate Western Europe, he would like to see Russia inherit the lead position.

June 9

I report to Paul and Gaby at Gaby's bedside. Into town to change money, etc. Then packing, lunch, and farewell.

By train to Paris. Past St. Quentin where the cathedral is still in the process of being built; Essigny le Grand where we went across the English trenches on March 24, 1918; Chauny, from where one always had to start out when going on leave; along the mountains of Sasigny where our division was wiped out; past the Oise-Canal. I feel that I am back in the war.

Arrive in Paris, I take a taxi to the Hotel Oxford et Cambridge. It is not expensive, but neither is it very Parisian.

Located near the Tuileries. I decide to stay only one night. First walk through the Tuileries, and along the Quai de Voltaire with its bookstalls. Beautiful, wonderfully beautiful. Dinner at Delpuech, opposite the Comédie Française, where I often ate in 1926. The price is still the same: sixty-six cents for three courses and a bottle of wine. I get into conversation with a cute girl from Nice who happens to be sitting next to me. My French begins to come loose at last. We ride to Montmartre together and, after trying unsuccessfully to get into a place where someone is singing chansons, we settle for a glass of vermouth with Seltz, which was my favorite drink in 1926. Then she leaves and I take a cab to the Grands Boulevards and the Café de la Paix, where I strike up a neighborly conversation with a girl from Alsace which further improves my French. As I walk home through the rue St. Honoré, an elegant car suddenly stops beside me and the lady at the wheel asks me for *"une allumette."* I express my regrets. Next she asks if I want to go nightclubbing on Montmartre with her, which I decline because of lack of money, to our mutual regret. Dead tired to bed.

June 10

Breakfast at a sidewalk café. Very nontourist, a delightful street scene. I look for another hotel and find an attic room at the Hotel St. Romain, rue St. Roche: 12 fr. instead of 22 fr.—about eighty cents a day.

I wander through the streets, past the stock exchange where the speculators are screaming their heads off. At one o'clock I meet Sabine Spiro. She has aged. Mendelsohn and Sabine want to get married as soon as possible. But they are not at all well off financially.

Home across the Place de la Concorde. Everything is incredibly beautiful under a soft sky that seems to dissolve into fluffy clouds.

I take care of some technicalities, letters, etc.; I have to change my clothes because the weather is so warm. At ten o'clock I am at the Place Pigalle, on Montmartre (having skipped dinner). Sabine Spiro comes for me and shows me one of many Montmartre cabarets. Everyone is dancing. Later there is a floor show featuring very nude girls. Police regulation: the girl must hold one hand over the decisive region. In between numbers they are very attractively and provocatively dressed. All this, with a glass of champagne, tips, etc., costs two dollars! I take a taxi (for half a dollar) back to my hotel after walking S.S. home. She lives at the very top of Montmartre.

June 11

At the Louvre: I visit the picture gallery only. But it is so overwhelming that I am at first more irritated than delighted. I spend a long time with the early Italians, including Cimabue and Giotto. I look at the frescoes, transferred intact, of Fra Angelico and Botticelli. In the center of the *grande galerie* are the six greatest works of all: the *Gioconda* (Mona Lisa), *St. Anne with the Virgin and Infant Jesus*; the *Concert Champêtre* by Giorgone; Raphael, and Titian. It almost takes one's breath away.

At one o'clock I meet Mendelsohn in front of a restaurant —which is closed. The strike of restaurant and café employees has begun. After several vain attempts at finding a place to eat, we turn into a side street where the restaurant owners' wives do their own cooking and are thus independent of the strike. Mendelsohn is old and ugly, quiet, but charming and very intelligent. After lunch he takes me through the old goldsmiths' quarter, a part of Le Marais, the section of Paris that has changed least over the years. He visits the shops with which he does business and where he is on friendly terms with the aging master craftsmen. He himself has taken his master's exam in Paris and makes his living executing small free-lance jobs in the jewelry field. His sister Anja is here, too. She works as a handwriting expert and psychologist. We discuss the strike with the master goldsmiths. Nobody seems to take the strike very seriously; some say that the government is actually behind the strike; others, that it is wrong to let the government down at this time. The pay is terribly low. There is a whole system of exploitation. Most of the people we talk to—café managers and workers—are Communists. They have completely accepted Mendelsohn. One of the master goldsmiths did all his gold-leafing for him free of charge—because he is a refugee.

Some *grévistes*—strikers—come up to us and ask for contributions. I contribute something—which may mean that I won't eat tonight.

Resting in my attic room, I call Mrs. Geiger (with whom we visited the Negroes in New York that time). We find a very good, inexpensive restaurant in Montparnasse. Mrs. Geiger has had a very hard time: her unhappiness in America has manifested itself in two serious illnesses which caught up with her in Paris, where she had to spend most of her time in the clinic. She still cannot drink wine.

We go to a French Negro nightclub. Different from Harlem. The Negroes here are not being persecuted for their race; they are more self-assured and more lascivious. At one o'clock the strikers force the owners to close down the place, so we miss most of the Negro high spirits.

June 12

At the Louvre. I get my bearings by writing down all the names that mean the most to me: all the great artists are here, with one or several of their greatest works. What I had remembered from 1926 was rather sketchy after all. I am now sitting in the Louvre garden beside a fountain, facing a view of the greatest and most magnificent palace in a vanishing world. It is very quiet and the soul fills with silence. At this moment the arc lights come on. I must stop. But once again

I know: man creates his world and there is none other—natural or supernatural.

At 12:30 the Riezlers come to my hotel. He looks older; she is as nice and elegant as ever. Both are full of warmth, delighted with my photos of René. We eat in a good French restaurant in the rue St. Anne. The main point of our conversation: they will not leave because of his mother-in-law, who has been utterly broken in spirit since Liebermann's death. I say that I cannot write a testimonial for his brother's book to which Furtwaengler has written the preface. That startles them somewhat. We talk about Heidegger, whom Riezler cut dead the last time they met. He also tells me that Werner Jaeger has been called to Chicago, that he has accepted, and that the Nazis are permitting him to go. He says that in today's Germany one can work only "beyond time." We leave all practical questions for another time. At the Café Napolitain we write a post card to the Reinhardts.

It is late in the afternoon, and I am a little tired. The restaurant strike is over. The workers and employees have won all kinds of concessions. After dinner I sit in a small restaurant in the Louvre garden, writing this. Today, after two weeks of waiting and beginning to get rather worried—some letters from Hannah at last. I cannot write to anyone: the complications of travel make everything impossible. I can only write this, and even this is not easy.

Late at night I visit Mendelsohn. His balcony faces south and overlooks the entire city. The Eiffel Tower still carries the "Citröen" sign, just as it did ten years ago. We share a bottle of Mousseuse. Mendelsohn is translating Goethe's *Prometheus* into French. He is also making a study of the French language which, in his opinion, is unique: it is the only language at which men have worked systematically for four hundred years, and which has thus grown into a miraculous work of art. It would take years for any one of us to learn to speak French so well that a Frenchman could bear to listen to us lecture in his *langue*. Mendelsohn calls my attention to still another element: French has continued the tradition of Latin in its pure form, whereas German had expelled its Latin components at the time of the mystics and Luther, thus separating itself from the European cultural tradition; which in turn has contributed to its rebarbarization.

I walk back to my hotel through the rue du Faubourg Montmartre, in the warm summer air.

June 13

I have my breakfast in bed, which doesn't cost any more than it would to have it at a café. To the Louvre garden where I am writing this and several urgent letters. Warm, gentle air; European clouds. At every hour of the day new beauties are revealed in the flowers, clouds, trees, and buildings. For lunch to good old Depuech's which is open once again. As I walk back to my hotel, I see someone limp across the sidewalk: Eckhart! I throw my arms around his neck right in front of everyone. I had not expected to see him until this afternoon, but he came as soon as he had arrived in Paris. He is staying at the house of an architect whose wife is a friend of his—outside the Porte de Versailles. He seems quite unchanged, has not aged, is only a little tired from traveling all night. We are happy. He was just going to lunch. I go with him, and we laugh as I have not laughed during this entire trip. He talks about his friend who is now in the Promised Land; about M. L. toward whom his feelings are always rather ambivalent; about his trip to Africa of which one never quite knows whether it will take place or not. We sit in the Café de la Paix for a long time. Then we go to his place, which entails a series of false starts since, of course, he does not have his house key. The house is tall and quite modern and has a lovely view of the castle of Mont Valérien and, beyond this, of St. Cloud and Versailles. The architect is a Hungarian who has succeeded in getting a foothold in Paris but is struggling, like all emigrants in Paris.

Eckhart takes a nap at my hotel while I spend another happy hour and a half writing letters in the garden. Later we stroll through the old streets, looking for a small place where a real Parisian might go to eat well and cheaply.

Our first political discussion. I describe the atmosphere and the ideas that prevail in the Western countries. He is for disarmament, and for acceding to Germany's "justified" demands; for reestablishing the position Germany had when she was an empire. He regards all attempts to stem the tide of European tragedy as pure utopianism, and withdraws into his individual concerns.

We cross the eastern boulevards on a bus; our goal is the rue de Lappe, one-time street of Apaches, where ten years ago Molla and I witnessed a battle between two streetwalkers. It has since become an amusement area for the *petite bourgeoisie*. A dark entrance, a house with closed shutters; a winding, narrow corridor; a large room with many men standing and sitting, and some very nude girls running around between them, offering their favors. We are told that there are forty girls in all. It is Saturday night, and the place is in full swing: soldiers, working men, *petits bourgeois,* some very old and some very young men, drinking beer and watching. Some disappear up the stairs, others come back down. A few of the girls talk to us. They are very nice about it and do not insist. After awhile they go away. On some Saturdays and Sundays there is dancing, too. We look in on yet another place—somewhat further down the social scale— and go home early.

June 14

I spend half an hour in the garden—the weather is wonderful. Then I go to meet Sabine Spiro at the Métro St. Paul for an official, paid, guided tour. Coming out of the Métro, I see and hear a street band playing the latest hit.

Because it is such a lovely day, only Mendelsohn, an old

99

lady, and myself are taking the tour; we head for the oldest part of Paris, a section that once belonged to the Order of the Knights Templar, and is now part of the Jewish quarter. In between, it was a residential section for the nobility. We see the Palais from which Anne of Austria watched Louis XIII enter Paris in triumph after his victory in the Fronde; the houses of Mme. Maintenon and Mme. Lamballe, Marie Antoinette's friend; the Temple Square where the king was imprisoned; a 500-year-old little street with a gutter running down its middle; the oldest Gothic house in Paris, etc., etc. It is a very worthwhile tour: these things are not easily found with a guidebook. On the Boulevard des Capucines I have a four-dollar dinner with wine—for sixty-six cents. Home to rest.

Ride to the Bois de Boulogne. A busy, bustling afternoon. Beautiful trees stand in visible air; one of the sources of French Impressionist painting. I sit for a long time, just looking. Everything here, every square, every park, every bridge, invites the eye because everything has been planned and shaped according to an original vision. The exaggerated visiting of art galleries and museums strikes me as inadequate because it is not truly dynamic.

A letter from Spiegelberg saying he has been dismissed and wants to see me in Geneva or Ascona. I write back, saying that I consider his dismissal a piece of good fortune.

At dinnertime I meet Frl. Dr. Rumpf of the Frankfurt Hochstift. She describes the virtual isolation in which intellectuals live in Germany; the changing ways of life, the status of women, the horrible military drill which brings about mechanization and atrophy of the will. She tells me about a law that declares that employees who have been divorced can be dismissed without pensions, and about the lack of freedom in the production of scholarly books which is more and more confined to the state-controlled publishing houses where practically every paragraph is subjected to censorship. We walk along the brilliantly illuminated boulevards. She radiates happiness at every step: to be out of there for a change; family reasons keep her in Germany.

I am tired out from the fresh air and all that walking. My rooftop room is beginning to be very hot, it is not good for summer.

June 15

To the Luxembourg garden. I visit the street and the hotel where I lived ten years ago. Everything is quite unchanged. The park is so lovely that I stay a long time, watching a little boy sail his toy boat on the pond. Behind the pond are flowers and trees, and over everything there curves the kind of sky that turns the whole thing into a dream picture of beauty.

At twelve o'clock, back to the hotel where Riezler calls for me. We eat at Weber's and talk for almost four hours. Of personal affairs: Werner Jaeger is going to Chicago; Reinhardt has become the *pièce de résistance* for good students in Frankfurt. Q is very unhappy, but not about world history, of which he notices nothing, but about their daughter's divorce. Hocher is somewhat old-maidish. On the general situation, Riezler says that the great majority of the people reject the Nazi philosophy completely; that the students are in full revolt; that they all take part in May Day demonstrations and keep on wearing corps colors to show their opposition. Krueger and Gadamer, Privatdozenten in Marburg, are not being promoted, he says, because their dossier contains the word *niveau*, meaning that their intellectual *niveau* is too high. He feels the regime has a low efficiency. There are many regions where it doesn't penetrate at all, for instance among the Bavarian peasants about whom he tells delicious anecdotes. But he thinks a collapse unlikely, unless Hitler were murdered by his own men, which he considers the safest solution. He sees the overall political situation in a very negative light, but feels that with a sensible government a

temporary solution could be found, even if it were to take the form of an armed truce. Unless something of the sort happens, he feels, war is inevitable. He himself has thought about the idea of a religious order from the Greek-humanist viewpoint: to gather together those who would carry on the tradition and thus save it esoterically. He fully agrees with the second, the humanist, element of my idea. He insists on the religious element becaues no truly esotric movement can exist without it. He thinks that there ought to be corresponding members, too, otherwise the whole thing would become too narrow. Furthermore, we discover a strong affinity between the Kairos doctrine and his ontology.

At 4:30 I am at the hotel, writing this. Late in the afternoon I walk to the Place de la Concorde. The light flows down the Champs Èlysées from the Arc de Triomphe, blinding the eye; I have to walk under the trees. After the sun sets, the sky glows golden through the curve of the Arc—as in an old painting. Later, to the Place St. Michel—and to a Restaurant Alsacien, which is famous for its good food. I drink some very tart Alsatian muscatel.

Down the Boul' Mich' through a crowd of students from the Sorbonne, to the Coupole on Montparnasse. Delightful atmosphere. Arabs, Turks, Negroes, all kinds of models, etc. I have an *apéritif* and am filled with happiness. Paris is the greatest temptation in the world. But all who have been tempted, especially the immigrants, become as miserable as Tantalus who sees all the splendors of the world and cannot grasp them.

June 16

I walk to the Orangerie—my hotel is quite centrally located—to see the Cézanne exhibit, and spend the entire morning hard at work.

I divide the hundreds of Cézannes into: landscapes; groups in landscapes; pure groups; portraits; and still-lifes. The landscapes are best of all because their style is mystic pantheism. The *Breakthrough*, a train going through a tunnel in a hillside, wins first prize from me, then come the Berlin and New York *Landscapes*. Also *La maison de l'homme perdu*. Among the groups in landscapes, the two most important items are *Les grandes Baigneuses* (with its slanting trees) and the *Battle of Life*. Among the pure groups: *The Card Players* and *The Pierrots*. Of the portraits, the "Self-Portraits" and the "New Yorker Self-Portrait." The finest still-lifes are those in which inorganic nature "lives." The French call it *nature morte*.

In my *Religious Situation* I wrote that a still-life by Cézanne has more religious quality than a *Jesus* by Uhde. That remark has often been quoted, and I still believe it is true. And yet, today I feel compelled to correct it. In the first place, the physical charm of the still-life is so tremendous because of its color—independent of content. And second: Cézanne proclaims a mystical devotion to life, and does so with the tools of a very great artist. Uhde proclaims ethical-social devotion with the tools of a minor artist. But basically he, too, is religious.

With Cézanne, landscape is all-important; everything less than landscape—the still-lifes, for instance—becomes landscape in his work. There is no *nature morte* in Cézanne—although he calls almost half his pictures just that. On the other hand, his groups and portraits, too, become landscape. His great self-portraits are views of "the fullness of being," not of a formed personality. And furthermore, the pictures are beautiful, and that is the main thing.

But not only the pictures—everything is beautiful: the rooms in which the pictures hang are themselves pictures. I had a similar experience in the *grande galerie* of the Louvre.

And the people, too, become pictures. There is, for instance, a perfectly picturesque middle-aged couple. Also, individual characteristics of Frenchmen and foreigners are fascinating to observe.

And outside, everything is all picture again. While I walk along the raised bank of the Seine, opposite the Quai d'Orsay, I feel that one would almost have to be negatively gifted *not* to be able to paint this.

Lunch at Léon, with especially good wine. The department stores are still closed. Trees, shimmering summer day. Deep sleep.

Through the Greek wing at the Louvre. There are few ancient originals, but some very beautiful Hellenistic and Roman copies. I ponder the facial expression of the gods. They are distant, self-contained, timeless, aloof from man and his humanity; whereas the pictures of the Christ show him in his nearness to man's helplessness.

To Notre Dame which is about to close. On the square behind the choir a crowd of people looks just like a scene from the Middle Ages, women nursing their babies, children and old people. Behind them rise the black-gray, gigantic buttresses of Notre Dame, and to either side flows the river.

Back to my hotel, then to Oldham's who is at the Hotel Royal. He is conducting a conference with several Protestant and Greek Orthodox bishops. I have a talk with Siegmund Schulze whom I expect to see again in Zurich.

Oldham invites me to dinner and a good bottle of wine. We talk about Brunner's anthropology. I am to write a brief critical review.

Eckhart and I meet at the Café de la Paix. I stroll through the rue Pigalle. Everything is too expensive. I end up at a corner café with a view of the busy streets. Pernod and Montanier—the famous *apéritifs*.

June 17

I call on Oldham. He takes me up to his room and once again we discuss the practical aspects of the religious-order idea. He is for an alliance of friends, which should produce a work center of its own on the one hand, while at the same time there should be recruitment among various congregations, groups, and political parties, for its ideas and aims. He then puts me through a kind of theological exam, and I am not quite sure whether I've passed it or not. He declares that, but for these two conversations with me, his stay in Paris would have been a waste of time.

Back to my hotel where Reizler sits waiting for me; Mrs. Riezler appears a few minutes later, and we go to eat in a little backyard restaurant.

Riezler's idea: to get rid of the dictator with the help of English money. He would like to see certain claims honored, and rearmament to continue on a moderate scale; he feels that negotiations with a reasonable government should be possible.

After a short rest at my hotel I meet Eckhart, and we eat in a small garden restaurant. Then we ride to the Bois where I meet Eckhart's hosts. He is a rather talkative architect, she a charming, clever historian who has not yet quite hit her stride. To the pond to watch the boats, torches, couples. We visit a café under the trees; music and thousands of people. Suddenly: a thunderstorm and rain. Eckhart and I return to the city. At the Café Weber we run into the Riezlers with a man from Frankfurt who knows me.

June 18

A busy morning on the telephone. Doering, who used to be union secretary in Frankfurt, calls on me. We meet at my hotel, then go to the Tuileries, and from there to Delpuech, where I invite him to lunch. He is in excellent shape, runs one of the "underground railways," talks about possibilities and impossibilities. He does not believe any real political effect is possible—but that personal convictions can and must be strengthened. We talk about Hagen, who is in New York and with whom his relations are somewhat strained. Since the "underground railway" depends on the old Party head and Second International for funds, they must be careful not to become suspected of Communism. He asks that Loewe and I work out a program, since no one quite knows what they are working for. Of personal matters, he reports that poor Stoffer has been nabbed. Quite certain that nothing can be done at the moment.

I wait till he finishes eating; then I go to Hugo Simon's office. He is successfully established in business here, after a year in Nice with his daughter, Mrs. Demeter. He has lost both his houses and all the money he had in Berlin, but says he does not regret it. He has saved his pictures, but not yet his books. He invites me to a good dinner, is as warm and cordial as an old friend. He has the same idea as Riezler: to get rid of the dictator and several others, to tear down the customs barriers, and to transform capitalism. His wife is in Nice. Demeter had first-rate reviews of his show here. What I have seen of his work is excellent. Simon has become heavier and grayer, but is as dignified and kindly as ever: Boas! He is optimistic about the inner-political situation in France, but very pessimistic about foreign policy, since the French don't want to acknowledge the threat from the East: he thinks a new "migration of people" is inevitable.

I ride to the Paris office of the Institute for Social Research, and then that nice Dr. Brill and I go to the Café Capoulade on the Boul' Mich'. The newspapers announce the following government decisions: dissolution of the rightist organizations; the forty-hour week; a subordination of the Bank of France to the government. Troops of students wander through the cafés, but laughter and cheerfulness prevail. Dr. Brill considers France a bulwark of anti-Fascism. The revolution of '89 cannot be undone, he says, while Frenchmen live. On the way back I run into Gurwitch, a student of Husserl's, who wants to go to America. I tell him in what low esteem phenomenology is held in America.

Back to the hotel. Eckhart comes to see me, straight from a visit to an ancient Princess Bonaparte who has written a three-volume work on Edgar Allan Poe. This book is not sold in Germany because of its "Jewish author."

We eat in the same little restaurant. By now they receive us with open arms. Eckhart works his way through a lobster. Afterward we pick up Mendelsohn and Spiro and visit a cellar place where the songs are partly witty and partly incomprehensible. Then on to a Negro bar, featuring interesting types.

June 19

Peace in the garden, after a bad night of inhuman heat. The water from the fountain wafts coolness across my face while I write.

Mrs. Kleyes calls for me at lunchtime. She has become somewhat rounder, is calmer and looks very well. We eat in a small Lyonnais place, excellent meal, her treat. She declares that no Frankfurt hostess can produce this kind of dinner any more. She tells me that her attitude remains unchanged, that she is thoroughly aware of the situation, through taking care of Fraenzel whom she has brought to London; that because of foreign exchange regulations, it is difficult to take care of him; that W. was a Nazi at first, but has gone further and further away from Nazism, partly because of what is happening and partly owing to her influence; that the Adlerwerkes are not getting any more war contracts because they are situated too close to the border; that after a tremendous industrial boom, the industrialists are now beginning to worry about what is coming next; that she herself is inwardly resigned, since her idealism has been shattered; that she helps many people and always speaks her mind very frankly; that W. is withdrawing more and more into hunting and racing; that he is incapable of writing letters, and that she herself no longer writes, since it is really impossible to write from Germany. I tell her about my ideas and about the situation, but I cannot convince her in any positive sense.

We go to the apartment of a French family, friends of hers, whose daughter she had looked after in Germany. They express the German attitude: against the Popular Front and sympathy with Hitler. This is the mood of the *bourgeoisie* when faced with the threat of a strike.

Back to my hotel. With Eckhart to the famous Maison des Nations (*maison d'amour de luxe*). Can be seen—for a few francs. Interesting rooms, gallery of beautiful girls. Only a prince can afford them—for the last eighty years—discretion! Dinner near the Porte St. Denis with Wagner-radio. Exploring old streets, including the rue de Lappe. Eckhart has to leave early, but I go on to the Dome and La Coupole. Plenty and Beauty. Life's ideal: to sit in a chair at a café in Paris.

I move my bed so that it stands betweeen the open window and the open door. It is terribly hot.

June 20

Sabine Spiro and I meet at the Gare de Montparnasse and we take the train to Chartres—via Versailles, Saint-Cyr, Rambouillet. We devote the entire day to Chartres Cathedral. Our first view is from outside—the Porte Royale. The open door draws you irresistibly toward the mystical stained-glass windows, which shimmer from a great distance behind the choir. The impression is tremendous and typically French: nave, choir, and all other parts have been fashioned with clarity and precision. The thirteenth-century windows are pure mysticism. Every window is a miracle in itself and must be studied in great detail. There are more than a hundred windows in all!! We spend an hour and a half, working with binoculars—and are hardly making any headway. For lunch —after walking out of a clip joint—we find an excellent truck drivers' inn, a place full of corners and nooks.

Back to the Cathedral. We alternate between inside and

outside. We look at the buttresses with their slanting columns and at the South Portal; the importance of blue in the windows; the long crypt.

Afterward we walk to the city gate and take the train back to Paris. Dinner at the Gare du Montparnasse. I stop briefly at my hotel, then go to visit the Café Maxville, where the Croix-de-Feux are staging a demonstration. A man offers the *Front Populaire* in a loud voice. I applaud and buy a paper from him—a kind of demonstration of my own.

June 21

Eckhart arrives after keeping me waiting for quite a while. Sunday excursion to the Marne. To the Chateau Vincennes and from there, by car, to Champigny. Charming river bath in the Marne. On the opposite bank there is a row of Corot trees. Green water. Everything is so very beautiful and well arranged. Although this is Sunday, there is an excellent crowd at the pool. A blonde from Hamburg with a Hungarian boyfriend, a Miss Basedow, knows many of our friends. She voluntarily left Germany in 1933 because she is a Socialist. We have some wine beside the pool in brilliant sunlight. Good conversation. Eckhart swims very well. Competition at the revolving swing: a delicately-built French girl wins over a sturdy German girl. Rain and thunderstorm. Walking along the Marne, I drink in the beauty of this landscape. Suddenly there appears Ida Berger, the little student from Frankfurt, with her husband and friends. Tremendous surprise! We make a date. The rain drives us into a restaurant beside the riverbank. While we wait for the rain to stop, we dance. By car to the subway. Eckhart and I eat dinner near the Madeleine.

I have a meeting with the Riezlers who have not yet left Paris. Important conversation about the possibility of finding one last rational criterion. For him, space and time are the basic categories of the structure of being. Problem: the relation of discoverable ontological structures of being to the structure of the criterion of revelation. Very warm mutual feelings. Anecdotes about the resistance of Bavarian peasants against the Nazis. Final farewells.

June 22

Many telephone calls. At ten o'clock Lieb calls for me and we walk to the garden, discussing the situation. He tells me that K. L. Schmidt wants to go to Vienna, that he feels too confined in Switzerland; and that Barth is very unhappy because there is no fertile soil for him there. That is how the "golden mountains" look at close range! Long live America! Lieb himself is going to reissue *Orient and Occident* which was ruined in Germany. He talks about developments in Russia where the Church is being given more freedom, but he feels that still more pressure should be exerted in this direction, in order to eliminate this particular objection the West can voice against Russia. He is very happy about the Front Populaire's election victory in France and considers France safe, although he recognizes the danger inherent in French backwardness and isolation. He cannot make up his mind whether or not to follow a call to Basel for next year. I advise him against it because of my idea about emigration. I explain my ideas on this subject to him, and he agrees wholeheartedly.

At lunchtime Professor Alexejef calls for me. He is writing the essay on Christian and Marxist anthropology in Berdyaev's place. I have read his outline which is rather good and am supposed to criticize it. Though he is an émigré, he is delighted with current developments in Russia. He feels they are partly due to the Russians' desire to disassociate themselves from Hitler. He is a "religious socialist" from his Russian days.

To Mme. Rappaport, now Perade. The Riezlers had given her my address. She has not been able to get her money out of Germany, and is now working hard for some fashion magazines. She is pretty as always, no longer paints her fingernails red. Recently she was the last person to be fired from a German magazine. Her editor-in-chief was not allowed to have any further contact with her. She wants to come to America, for her own sake and especially for the sake of Beckmann who has been utterly crushed in Germany.

To Mrs. Kleyes' where Eckhart awaits me. We all go to one of the big cafés on the Champs Èlysées. Mrs. Kleyes tells me about an evening with Picasso and others, all enthusiastic followers of the Front Populaire as she assures me. All leftist France is in a fever of expectation, whereas the rightists are frightened and are taking their money out of the country. The strike was a little revolution. The employees had barricaded themselves inside the buildings, behind lowered shutters, and it never even occurred to the government to send in the police. At night the men slept in the buildings and the women brought food to them. Blum is greatly respected, but there are doubts about his leadership qualities.

The sun burns through my suit and irritates the slight sunburn I contracted at the Marne pool; a veil seems to cover my eyes and ears; I rarely get more than four hours' sleep a night. But I can still answer when someone speaks to me— a peculiar feeling of fading away.

We visit Serves, the publisher of the *Cahiers d'Art*, an impressive head. I ask about Mrs. Bienert and learn, to my amazement, that she has told him everything would be over within a year: a complete reversal of attitude. Eckhart and I wonder whether this is fact or tactics.

We go to Montparnasse. At Mrs. Geiger's hotel I am told that she has gone to the clinic. Dinner with Eckhart who has moved into my hotel at last in order to be a little more independent of his hosts.

After dinner we stroll through Montparnasse; even the riddle of the Sphinx is quickly solved during a downpour. By car to the hotel, then to the Gare du Nord. We say good-by over a glass of champagne. I treat him to a nightcap. We part with heavy hearts. Afterward I walk for a long time through familiar and unfamiliar streets in the northern section of Paris.

June 23

Ida Berger arrives at my hotel at ten o'clock. We go directly to the Châtelet where I have an appointment with Benjamin, who gets there much too late. Ida Berger sits down to work at another table.

I explain my ideas to Benjamin; he says they go right to the heart of the matter, they are Columbus' egg. But it may be too late; everything might well have to be destroyed first. He is particularly interested in the problem of esoterism in the spiritual dimension. Eckhart had objected, calling it a synthesis of various elements, not a new principle.

With I. Berger to the hospital to visit Mrs. Geiger who is confined to her bed for several more weeks. I meet Mrs. Lobernheim there, the mother of Lobernheim who visits us occasionally.

With I. Berger, who is expecting a baby, to the Place de la Concorde. From there to Hugo Simon's. She tells me that she is married to a laborer, has become a French citizen, teaches at the Workers' High School, and has settled happily into her life. She says her husband is charming. She says she owed her methodical education entirely to my seminars.

In Simon's entrance hall I meet the writer Siemssen. The three of us ride to the Seine Island and have lunch in a restaurant called Chez Paul in an old square. When we want to order the same wine twice, the restaurateur becomes indignant and declares that we must order Beaujolais with the meat. We comply.

Our conversation develops in three directions: Siemssen wants to gather all anti-Fascist forces into the framework of the Popular Front; Simon wants to work against the Fuehrer

in social-revolutionary style, i.e., with daggers and bombs; and I explain the idea of the religious order; this impresses Simon so greatly that he wants to arrange a conference for August, when I come back to Paris.

I see Sabine Spiro very briefly. She seems a bit less tired.

Mrs. J. calls for me. We talk for about three hours, walking mostly under the Rivoli and Vendome colonnades while lightning flashes across the sky and thunder growls.

Then dinner in a little restaurant. She declares categorically that she will have nothing to do with V., Mr. J's. new wife, and the same goes for the children. I admit that love cannot be commandeered, but I also insist that some arrangements must be made to protect him from being emotionally and spiritually torn; for instance, a definite schedule for visiting the children ought to be established. I insist further that she should recognize the new marriage as valid, as a real marriage, due to his decision. She is not yet ready for that. She suffers a great deal, does not look well and feels unhappy in Paris, like most of the others. She tells heart-rending stories about refugees in Paris: judges selling books from door to door, lawyers delivering milk and vegetables; a rash of suicides.

I take her to the bus stop. Afterward, a most beautiful walk between nine and ten o'clock at night; from the Louvre, through the Tuileries, across the Place de la Concorde, along the Champs Èlysées, to the Rond Point. Illuminated fountains everywhere. In the background, the Arc de Triomphe, bathed in floodlights. Over it all, the afterglow of the evening. Everything is infinitely beautiful.

At the Rond Point Café I meet Lucie Bieber. She has lived here three years and is doing quite well as a gymnastics teacher. Her husband is not doing nearly so well, and their money will soon run out. They are not happy in Paris and would actually like to go to America where being a refugee is quite different from what it is in France. Always the same story.

She has aged, her features are somewhat sharper, her hair

is gray, but she is still good-looking. She tells me that a friend has just lost her second lover because of the race laws.

Back to the nocturnal Seine. First good night's sleep, thanks to the cooler weather.

June 24

Up early—and a long time packing. At the American Express office where I've gone to arrange about my ticket, I meet Professor Spann from Chapel Hill.

I finish packing, then go to have my last lunch in Paris, with champagne *naturel*. By train to Basel—second class for six dollars!! Hot and tired. The train hurtles through a heavily wooded landscape. I have been writing this for the last four hours. Paris was incredibly rich, day after day, from the 9th to the 24th, from 8:00 A.M. to 2:00 at night, and I enjoyed it all with intense awareness. Since I had to alternate between seeing people and seeing the city for its own sake, this visit was not as serenely relaxed as the one I paid ten years ago, but this time the experience was far more intense, more real, more conscious. And the beauty of that most beautiful of cities has remained unchanged.

We ride through valleys of fragrant meadows. Hay is being carried on carts drawn by oxen or horses; there is no automobile in sight for five hours. The stormy evening lends marvelous colors to sky and earth. Dinner with a final bottle of French wine.

Arrival in Basel. Customs. K. L. Schmidt waits in the background. By train to Riehen, a tip of Basel that is surrounded on three sides by Germany. Uncanny feeling, like being pushed into a sack. The nearest lights are German, the streetcars cross the border; a German narrow-gauge train with German officials runs past the house.

I have left K. L.'s briefcase somewhere. Back the way we came: find it at the station's Lost and Found Department. Beer in a garden where people are dancing. First talks. He might be called to Vienna. His wife is in the hospital again. She has been in bed for months, keeps having relapses. A former theology student who had studied under him and Hoelscher, now Mrs. Emmerich (married to a Jewish refugee) runs their household. She appears as we arrive at his house. She is ugly in a funny way, but intelligent and alert. The Basel air makes me deathly tired.

June 25

Fatigued despite long sleep. Spend the morning in the garden, sorting letters; arrange tomorrow's schedule by telephone. Lunch with Mr. and Mrs. Emmerich and K. L. and two of the children. I am continually tired.

To town with K. L. We try in vain to visit Mrs. Schmidt; she has just had another relapse. We get a ride back in the car of an admirable religious-socialist pastor who has read everything I've written. After dinner he drives us to the Baumgartens' who are giving a reception for me. Baumgarten looks older. She is pretty and wide-awake as always. About twenty people arrive, among them Menk and Sewald, many very fine heads. No ladies. After punch with strawberries, I have to speak on the problem of "The Tragic and the Ethical" in the present situation. Strong impact, especially on Sewald and Baumgarten. The latter says that my lectures have given him strength. Apparently he feels very much alone. One of the participants in the discussion defends England. Menk speaks about the necessity of the religious-order idea. Home by car. Overall impression: deepest pessimism everywhere.

June 26

In conversation with Mrs. Emmerich I learn that the Swiss Foreigners' Police is turning into a kind of budding Gestapo, which may be important in times to come.

At 11:30, at Karl Barth's. Extremely animated friend-to-friend conversation in which we trade insults. I tell him about Barth in America whereupon he declares that under the circumstances he won't have to go there. I say that, unlike him, I feel closer to the early Christians than to the Reformation; that, for me, the criterion is all-important; that I feel his letter contradicted his theology. To which he can only add that he could not have done otherwise three years ago. He feels my existence in America is providential. We part as great friends.

From Barth's directly to the Baumgartens' for lunch. We talk of personal matters. Baumgarten had studied Russian for three years, then spent some very intensive weeks in Russia and is now practically rooted in Communist soil. Feels very lonely. We talk about the chances of my taking a trip to Russia. He could help me a lot.

They never received Hannah's poems, which went instead to the Old Testament scholar, Baumgartner, whom we know from Marburg.

On to Sewald's, who is rather unhappy about the narrowness of Swiss academic life. I try to make him see his role of immigrant in a more positive light.

To the hospital to see Mrs. Schmidt. She looks dangerously thin and transparent. I have a short, lively talk with her. As always, we agree in our basic ideas.

I meet Ministerialdirektor Richter. He gives me his view of the situation; it sounds even more hopeless than mine. He says that things of unimaginably low morality are continuously happening. He feels the universities are dead, transformed into mere cadet training grounds. He thinks that war is inevitable. He was at the Baumgartens', too, last night, taking part in the discussion. He does not believe in a militarist-monarchist solution. He himself is studying theology in Basel, lives near the border because of his pension, has to cross the border twice a day. He is very unhappy about Eric Seeberg, predicts he'll come to a tragic end someday, considers him politically inept and feels that he was most recently under the influence of his father.

To Menk's, who invites me for dinner. Excellent conversation about psychoanalysis and religion, especially the problem of whether the power to fulfill his own meaning is inherent in man. He postulates that every human being brings a "program" into the world, whose fulfillment is, at the same time, the fulfillment of the meaning of his life. We call for his wife at the theater, walking through ancient streets. She has white hair but seems young. We cross the Rhine and walk past nightspots full of soldiers and students who sing and drink wine: Europe!

I go back to Schmidt's and we talk until two in the morning, over a bottle of good Swiss wine. I am astonished to discover that Schmidt has reverted to a primitive orthodoxy of inspiration; so has Mrs. Emmerich. He considers the virgin birth a photographically demonstrable fact; the same with the rest of the miracles, because the Bible says so—such as the empty tomb and others. I can only think: my predictions have come true even faster than I expected.

June 27

Pack and leave for Zurich. By car to the Medicuses'. They live very agreeably in a house of their own, surrounded by a flowering garden. From the balcony in front of my room I see Lake Zurich. Frede calls. He and Trudchen have been living at the Pestalozzis' for the last few days. We arrange to meet at the Café Odéon, my usual meeting place in Zurich.

They seem quite unchanged and are very sweet. We discuss our travel plans, talk about this and that, without touching on anything basic.

As I walk through the café, I suddenly find myself face to face with Hirschfeld, the friend of Emmy Sachs who used to be Intendant in Darmstadt, then went to Zurich, and is now working for Oprecht Publishers. We decide to get together on Sunday night.

Trudchen, Frede, and I walk to a new restaurant with a view of the lake. Trudchen is feeling much better. But both have to take it easy because of their hearts. They report that my beloved father is not really ill; it is a hysterical disturbance. The doctors have pronounced him in perfect physical health.

Dinner in an Italian restaurant with "bandits" and a beautiful, fat Italian woman. I walk Trudchen and Frede to the railroad station, then stroll through the town and finally ride back to the Medicuses'. He is happy to be a Swiss citizen, to have freed himself completely from Germany.

He talks about his children. They are very musical. Two of them, a son and a daughter, want to become opera singers, which worries their parents. Medicus himself had just come from the Bruckner festival. For him, music is the highest form of fulfillment.

June 28

To Mrs. v. Bendemann's. She lives rather shabbily in exile with her son. Her works can no longer be published. She has suffered a severe illness. We talk about Mrs. Goldstein who wrote to her about having talked with me. I explain it all, and Mrs. v. Bendemann agrees with my ideas and promises to write to Mrs. Goldstein to that effect. We take a streetcar to the station. A young girl comes up to me. She turns out to be Leni Buri, the funny little girl at the Salis' house. We travel together for ten minutes. She has become older but not much more sensible.

At the Oberrieden station Frede awaits me in Pestalozzi's car. Drives me to their country house—straight into paradise. View of the lake and the Alps. Wonderful garden, bordering on a forest. A simple meal with many children and good wine. Afterward Frede and I stretch out in deck chairs. Pestalozzi takes long trips and has taken beautiful photographs of which a book has now been published. He sees the existence of Switzerland as being problematic. Would like to combine the French part of Switzerland with France and says there is a strong tendency toward such a move. Frede says he is the "chauffeur" of Barth. He takes me to Kilchberg by car. There, on the shore of Lake Zurich, Leni Buri's parents have a magnificent house. They receive me very cordially.

After a visit to Conrad Ferdinand Meyer's grave, I take a streetcar to the Odéon to meet Hirschfeld. We eat in a nice old place where the sound of the Sunday evening bells is so overpowering that one can hardly talk. Later we discuss various books published by Oprecht on which he (Hirschfeld) has worked. At the moment the most important—though not the best—is *I Cannot Keep Silent*. His work on Langhof's *Moorsoldaten* consisted in taking out the most gruesome parts and placing the beautiful passage about the prisoners' theater in the center of the book. He was also instrumental in getting Langhof across the border. He himself was in Russia for a long time, studying the Russian theater. This brought him into close contact with the Russians; Eisenstein wanted to keep him there. But he preferred to stay in his embattled position in Zurich. He seems to have many underground connections. We walk back and forth on the Limmat Bridge, with the moon and thousands of lights across the lake. Later we sit in a beer garden where a band plays a medley of German songs. At ten o'clock we go to Medicuses'. Sitting beside an open window wall, we drink two bottles of wonderful wine. Medicus and Hirschfeld have a lively conversation about—I think—the world situation. But the moment is much too beautiful to be reminded about it.

June 29

I work on my lecture, in the garden. Salome Boller calls for me and we go for a walk together. She has been almost continually sick, but looks better than she did. She cannot leave, since she is her family's only support.

Lunch at the Medicuses'. The very vivacious singer-daughter appears and is grateful when I say that she seems to have the right temperament for the stage.

Work on my lecture. To the Odéon, where Georgy Frey-Sollberger, an old school friend of Johanna's, is waiting for me. She has joined the Oxford Movement (Buchman), knows Brunner, and very enthusiastically describes the spiritual power that emanates from there. She seems very calm and serene. Her life has taken on direction, and she does much good. All decisions are made by community meditation. The superiors' decisions must be obeyed. She describes Buchman as short, fat, and not very attractive.

To Siegmund-Schulze's house. He lives on the mountain, has an incredible view over the lake and the Alps. He left Germany when he got a hint from the Foreign Office that there was no way of shielding him. He confirms my general impression of Switzerland.

It is pouring as I ride to the university. Lecture on "Protestantism and the World Situation." My analysis makes a deep impression on the large, excellent audience. My concrete suggestions have no noticeable effect. Two Rotarians, Julius Lehmann and Albert Hahn, are in the audience. Also, there is the art historian, who tried in vain to become a lecturer under Jantzen, with his beautiful Jewish wife who once had a photo studio in the Kaiserstrasse. Of course, the Fredes, the Pestalozzis, Georgy, Hirschfeld, Bendemann, and the Medicuses are there. Also Brunner, the Bollers, etc. Long discussion afterward. First, a very cordial debate—almost tinged with personal warmth—with Brunner about my theological position. Then with Medicus about the esoterics. Hahn adds a question on economics. After the discussion, to Julius Lehmann's. He left Germany right away and so was able to get all his money out. He lives in a very beautiful place, has a car. His wife was there, too. He offers me a sum of money for myself and for the refugees. I accept. Albert Hahn, who did not come along, was charming. But he said he would not be in Ascona in August because his wife is expecting a baby.

June 30

Packing, telephone calls—for instance, to good old Wendriner who was at my lecture, too, where he had told me briefly about Hannah's birthday party.

Departure for Berne. I talk to a Swiss woman who owns the bookstore in the Basel railroad station. She describes the way Germans act when buying books that are forbidden in Germany: with fear and trembling. Hirschfeld told me that a German public prosecutor sometimes comes to visit him here, to spend the night breathlessly reading through the newer books.

At the station I meet the Blums and Wolfers who are taking the same train as far as Geneva. The Blums have a new apartment with partial view of the Bernese Uplands. Around the corner, view of the Alps with the Jungfrau in the center. After lunch we walk through beautiful old Berne with its arcades reminiscent of Bologna, its patrician town houses, and the bridges from which you see the Alps.

To the travel agency. Along the Aar River which is full of wild glacier water.

I change, dine, then go to my lecture. A small but select group has assembled. The students, reticent at first, are so impressed that they offer to get me further lecture engagements—in Geneva, etc. During the discussion period I run into strong theological opposition from strict Barthians. But the younger ones are on my side.

July 1

I repack everything in order to take only two suitcases to Italy. Departure for Zurich—St. Moritz. In Zurich-Thalwit,

Frede and Trudchen board the train. Marvelous ride via Chur to St. Moritz. On the train, Mr. and Mrs. Berlepsch, of the Leipzig seminar, who are now living in Zurich; also two schoolteachers from Gaben who had brought me greetings from a group in Gaben after my lecture in Zurich.

We get off the train in pouring rain. Hotel Zur Post in St. Moritz. Frede and Trudchen take a magnificent room with a view of the lake. Dinner for five Swiss francs. Walk in the rain through the village. Early to bed.

July 2

It is pouring. Short walk up the mountain between two showers. At eleven o'clock I take the bus to Sils Maria and go straight to the Salises'. Mrs. Salis recognizes me when I mention Loewe. We order lunch and walk over to the Fextal gorge: water from below, from above, from everywhere.

Lunch at the Salises' is as delicious as it was the last time; we eat on a newly added porch with a view of the Maloia. Suddenly at four o'clock, blue sky from Maloia. Grandiose battle scenes in the sky, clouds and sun in combat. The Margna emerges. Snakes of mist on the slopes of the Lagrev. Prolonged battle for the Lunghin. Radiant blue sky over Italy. Mrs. Salis brings out all the old pictures of Erdmuthe. As we start to leave, we meet a family from Berlin named Seligsohn, in the foyer. They know me from the Netters', and I learn from them that Mrs. Netter died a few months ago.

Then, up on the Chasté which is magnificent "as on the primal day." Full view of the Fextal. I visit every single spot. Back via Sils Baseglia. Dinner at the Salises'. Back to St. Moritz by bus. Moonlight on the lake.

July 3

We take a trip through Gamaden into the Lower Engadine. View of the Palue and Bernina. By bus through the Ofental.

Short rest below the Ofenpass. Down into the Vintschgau. Italian border inspection. We wait in little villages, in full view of the Ortler Group. By bus to St. Valentino alla Muta. Wide, fertile valley with lakes and incredible view of the Ortler, Koenigspitze, etc. Tall, wooded mountains rise to the right and left; the slopes of the Oetztal Alps to the east, smaller ranges to the west. To the north lies the Reschen-Scheidegg which leads into the Lower Engadine and Austria.

There are Italian soldiers everywhere.

Elisabeth and Erhardt, and somewhat later, M. L., arrive at the hotel. They have an apartment with view of the Ortler —a whole floor to themselves, with a separate room for each, and a common living room. We eat in a simple restaurant with good Tyrolean wine and uninteresting food. Elisabeth is tanned and very happy, Erhardt still a bit tired. M. L. on top of the world, as usual. Everything is in excellent shape.

I have talked with Frede and Trude day after day. Trudchen is desultory and a convinced National Socialist; Frede more critical but full of hatred against foreigners and refugees, especially Jews. Conversation is very difficult because of the way Trudchen jumps from one subject to another. I can talk about a number of issues with Frede, but not with Trudchen. Elisabeth is infinitely more objective and easier to get along with. Erhardt is very quiet. All behave in a somewhat pedagogical way toward me. M. L. is silent.

Marvelous red sky over the Ortler Group. Tired—early to bed.

July 4

Breakfast in bed, to the accompaniment of the great, roaring waterfall. Long walk through wonderful forest with Elisabeth. She is sweet and serious and objective. It feels like the old days.

Lunch under a sun umbrella. Erhardt and I climb a mountain on the other side of the woods; it is a very difficult climb; there are Alpine roses. Elisabeth and M. L. stay behind. Frede and Trudchen have not come along. My first test and training, still without climbing boots.

Dinner with cake and white Chianti. Moon over the mountains.

July 5

I am working in the woods; on my diary, on some letters. The air is balmy and there is an infinity of flowers; the meadows have not been mowed yet. I have a touch of lumbago and am stretched out in a chaise lounge facing the Ortler Group. Later I walk around the lake which reminds me of the Silvaplana Lake. Cornfields full of corn flowers. After dinner, at home, there is a general discussion about anthropology.

July 6

We get up at 5:30 A.M. All except Trudchen walk up the Zwoelfer Kogel (9,000 feet). Frede slowly walks ahead through woods to the pasture and hut. It is very hot. We have some milk in the hut, then begin the first climb in the sun. M. L. wants to turn back, then changes her mind and stays with us. We climb up through snow fields; I am the one who puts down the trail. M. L. and Elisabeth have moments of terror. We three men continue up to the ridge, a very steep climb. Then I go back for the women, supporting them in word and deed. Erhardt and I climb to the top, along a steep ridge. At the summit, infinite beauty.

A thunderclap. Down in a hurry. The three others have already started down toward the Ray Valley on the other side. Rain. We traverse some snow fields and find shelter in a low hut. Then for several hours we walk through a long valley in the burning sun. From there, mortally exhausted, by car to the Traube in Valentino. Drink—drink and food. This has been a real Alpine tour. Totally depleted, to bed.

July 7

I get up tired. There is a moist wind from the south. Work. A violent discussion with Trudchen on National Socialism. My bones ache with fatigue. After lunch I take a long rest, later I study the Ortler Group. I receive a letter from Hannah.

Am writing and dictating some letters, then I take a beautiful walk in the rain. After dinner I report on my discussions in England, etc.

July 8

It rains during the night. I dictate letters to M. L. all morning, sitting on stones and benches. Rainy afternoon, which I spend sorting letters. The others are reading the books I have brought along, about Hitler, concentration camps, the mood in Germany, etc.

Earlier, at lunch, we had an explosion over the Jewish question and the boycott. I identify myself with the fate of the Jews. In the evening I read my program outline aloud. Discussion, especially over the section on foreign policy. That night I have a ghastly dream: my eyes are going to be put out. Next morning M. L. analyzes my dream as stemming from a sense of aggression from the family.

July 9

Rain and fog. Analytical discussions with M. L. I dictate letters until 5:00 P.M. Suddenly there is a thunderstorm; the clouds are torn apart. Wonderful blue of the Ortler Group, mixed with blinding white. We take a walk along the Etsch River which is full to overflowing. From a meadow we see across valleys, fields, and mountains. In the evening we say good-by over Asti Spumante.

July 10

Elisabeth, Erhardt, and I ride to Gulden, in the middle of the Ortler Range, 4,000 feet high, very famous. The three others are to follow later. It is sunny at first, then overcast. The trip is complicated: first by bus, then in a private automobile, then by bus again. Magnificent, frightening drive through breakneck curves, just as it begins to rain. Lunch at the Post Hotel, after a prolonged search at the Hotel Tembl; the hotel is wonderfully well situated in the upper part of the valley with a view of the Ortler Group and the Gulden glacier.

Erhardt and I walk through the black-pebbled Schluntal from Gulden up to the glacier moraine. There is snow everywhere. We hike back over black rocks in pouring rain. Comforted by Vino Moscato and a game of chess with Elisabeth. Fruitless attempts to reach Frede by telephone.

July 11

My telephone call reaches Frede at last. He would prefer to go to Riva on the Lago di Garda, but agrees to come here instead. Elisabeth and I take a walk along the western slope of the Ortler Range. Sun and rain.

In the afternoon, with Erhardt to the Kanzel, "Il Pulpito," all signs are in Italian. Through a most beautiful forest with larches and a wonderful reddish kind of fir tree. The last tree, far, far away from the others, stands ragged in the fog.

On to the Pinao Rosim, an old frontal moraine which is now overgrown and wonderfully situated in the Rosim Valley, from where we have a view of the surrounding mountains and glaciers. Ortler and Koenigspitze are beautifully visible. Constant change between shrouding fog and clear views, results of the "divine Reinhardt." The intensely blue-green Rosim glaciers, the gentians and mountain anemones, and everywhere the meadows are red with alpine roses. We descend through fog. The other three, Frede, Trudchen, and M. L., arrive. They are very critical, which infuriates Elisabeth. I make peace between them. Reconciliation over glasses of Moscato. Rain, rain—early to bed.

July 12

Fresh snow, then rain: the barometer is rising. I have breakfast while everyone else is still asleep. The Fredes and Seebergers go to church, while M. L. and I walk up to the end of the Gulden glacier: it is very high, a smoothly cut-off mass, dirty, covered with stones. Great stone avalanches prevent our getting closer. The Gulden Brook gushes out of a green cave. Some snow comes drifting down. In the valley it is raining.

We all take a beautiful, easy walk in the afternoon, through the woods, with view of the mountains of the Lower Engadine. Sunday afternoon, coffee house with nothing but Germans. M. L. and Trudchen stay behind, sitting in fields of alpine roses. We others keep going. Wonderful walk back. The Ortler has come into full view. Later, in Frede's room, we have a good talk about the authority of the Bible. I go to bed very tired; I can never really get to sleep here without taking some Baldrian.

July 13

A long walk to the Schanbach (now Mailaender) hut. Pleasant, slow climb. We catch up with Trude and Frede who have started out way ahead of us. We make it in somewhat less than two hours. Trudchen manages to get there, too. Lunch in the hut, then M. L. and Trudchen get stowed away in deck chairs. We others climb up the Hintere Schoentaufspitze, 9,000 feet—as high as the Julier. For two hours we are almost continually in snow. Then a steep climb over rocks. At the top, indescribable fog images with changing colors. Down in the rain. We all go to bed dead tired.

July 14

A day of rest. We sit in deck chairs, interrupted now and then by showers. Letter from Hannah to M. L. In the afternoon we walk to the Grand Hotel from where we have a fine view of the Koenigspitze. Erhardt falls on the parquet floor. We walk in the direction of the Duesseldorfer hut. M. L. disappears and does not come back. We worry about her. She reappears around eight o'clock; she had gone off because we talked too much theology. Everyone cusses her.

The mountains in the evening . . .

July 15

To the Payer hut. I have my toothbrush in my knapsack, just in case. Trudchen stays behind, Frede comes with us as far as the timberline.

We march across pebbly slopes at the foot of the Ortler. Under the pebbles lies the glacier. M. L. is astonished at the untidiness in nature. Steep climb to the Tabaretta hut. Sheep in snowy fields.

Pea soup and Kaiserschmarren in the hut. An old woman and a shepherd boy wait on us.

Elisabeth and M. L. keep asking everyone we meet for the right way, until, in the end, they become discouraged and don't want to go on. Vain attempt to get M. L. across the first snow field on the slope. Elisabeth turns back, then follows us; I go back to get her. Climb up a steep slope to the crest. Sheep are causing stone avalanches. On the crest we have a magnificent view of the Stilfser Jochstrasse as far as the shelter.

Narrow path up a steep, rocky slope. Elisabeth gropes about her, and I have to hold her. The hut is like a medieval castle on a steep rock, right up against the summit glaciers of the Ortler. The summit is in the clouds; there is a strong, very cold, westerly wind.

We have tea and wine in the hut. I decide reluctantly to give up the idea of climbing the Ortler next morning. Our descent is accompanied by thunder which might be caused by lightning, or else by stone avalanches. Elisabeth is quite excited, but brave. M. L. is very unhappy after having waited for us at the Tabaretta hut for four hours. We climb down through the rain.

July 16

I get ready to leave; the weather is wonderful and warm. I take a short walk up the slope. All the mountains are in view, especially the unbelievably beautiful Koenigspitze. To the Zag Valley, up to the timberline. Despite yesterday's exertions, I feel perfectly fit. Have become quite used to the altitude and am ready for any sort of climb. Instead, I pack, and at five o'clock in the afternoon, take the bus to Spantigna. View of the Geisterspitze. By train through the fertile Vintschgau, to Meran. View across the Leaser and Mantell valleys toward our old mountain peaks. Vineyards, castles, chestnut trees; the ancient part of town; heat.

In Meran I stay at the Hotel Baviera. Dinner in the garden under palm trees, flowering oleander and laurel. A short walk, dance music. Arbor street. Wine in the garden. Late to bed. I lie awake until 4:30 because of the heat and the wine.

July 17

A nice breakfast in the garden. I have to do some errands in town. The Passeier Brook, quick, strong, and cool; the old trees; mountains all around the town, some of them snow-capped.

With Frede and M. L. to the Lido. We swim in full view of the mountains, as we did in Ascona and Menaggio. Lunch at Duano. All the ladies buy gloves.

By car to the Tyrol Castle. Very interesting reliefs, some

dating back to the ninth century; struggle between paganism and Christianity. Frescoes. Fantastic view through the early-Romanesque windows. Long rest in the grass. The vegetation here is the same as in the Burgell. Reminiscent of Solio. We return through a valley whose vegetation reminds me of the Giardsue near Mentone, with a racing mountain brook added.

Dinner at the Stilvio. At the next table there are about thirty students from Tübingen, with their teachers. They are on a geographic excursion. I find myself beset by strong, regressive excitement. We talk about science and the Nazis. They have read Heiden's book about Hitler with passionate interest; also some books about concentration camps. They reject them, but are impressed nevertheless.

To the main promenade where there is a great deal to see. The ladies retire. Frede and I have an Orvieto (Bigi) in honor of our impending separation. We feel very close as human beings. This morning I took Erhardt to the train. We love each other very much. He is one of the most decent people I know, has remained a member of the Confessing Church. At times the Confessing Church suffers from dogmatism to the point of intolerance, especially among the students, while the leaders often suffer from arrogance. Between Elisabeth, who belongs to the Confessing Church, and Erhardt, who has suffered greatly on its behalf—and Frede, who never belonged to it—there is a certain tension which leads to occasional outbreaks. But in all instances, as with me, too, the old human bonds have proved stronger than the very obvious and clearly defined objective differences.

July 18

Our last breakfast together. Back to the hotel and to the railroad station. Parting from Frede and Trude. Nowadays one always wonders: "Is it forever?"

I work in the park. Then lunch with Elisabeth and M. L.

I write some letters in the restaurant, which happens to be the only cool place I can find.

To the Lido. The only possible thing to wear: a bathing suit. To the fruit market. The only possible food: fruit.

By tram to Ober-Mais. Walk through grape arbors—to the Restaurant Valentino. Oleander and chestnut trees. Climbing over fences. An old woman runs the place. We ride back, and M. L. goes to bed. Elisabeth and I, alone, say good-by to each other.

It is a very sweet, personal conversation. We discuss the problem of Trudchen. Tension between her and Gisela. Growing tension between Elisabeth and Frede, despite their closeness, because of Frede's negative attitude to things in general and toward the Confessing Church in particular.

July 19

Up early. Elisabeth takes me to the bus. Difficult leave-taking. Ride from Meran to Bolzano through burgeoning landscape with vineyards and many mountains.

I have ten minutes in the Cathedral of Bolzano while Sunday services are being held there. Then the ride continues through a long, smooth valley with a few deep gorges to the Casazza Pass. Magnificent dolomite formations, green mountain lake. Down, then up again to the Pordoi Pass. Ever new, fantastic architectural groups of dolomites.

As I arrive at the Pass, there is Claire in a yellow dress; also Guenther and the children. They have come to call for me in the hotel car. Claire is very pretty. Guenther has aged a little. He wants to address me in the formal "you" form. I immediately call him "thou."

They have brought lunch along. Peter walks ahead—and disappears. We go after him in the car; then turn back for him. Great excitement. Finally we continue on our way—and catch up with him two villages farther on.

It is a wonderful trip. More and more new groups of mountains come into view. Red and blue are the basic colors of earth and sky here. Down to Cortina after yet another mountain pass. All this is only four hours by bus from Venice! Arrival at the Hotel Cristallo, a big luxury hotel. I am given a room with a balcony on the first floor, which looks out on a magnificent group of dolomites. The hotel is overcrowded. Only one room is available because a friend of Mrs. Badoglio, the wife of the victor of Ethiopia—Duke and Viceroy—is expected in a few days.

On the terrace, Sunday coffee is served, and a band plays. I change and come down. Suddenly the hotel station wagon arrives and brings M. L., who had gone to Franzensfeste with Elisabeth in order to make use of her ticket and has now come here by a different route. Coffee with Claire and M. L. Down below, there is a tennis tournament. Music, sunshine, swimming pool, mountains.

We take M. L. to the Pension Serena. Dinner with the children and a great international crowd. Many Italian aristocrats. Mother and daughter Badoglio, Duchess of Aosta, etc. Half Italian, half German; the Germans half Nazi, half anti-Nazi, which has led to splits and clashes.

To the tavern, where the prizes for the tennis tournament are being handed out. Dancing. At our table, two ladies from the Berlin world of sports—members of the aristocracy. Boring. Everything very international. In addition to the basic German and Italian stock, there are Hungarians, Americans, Egyptians, Austrians, Frenchmen. Many children. I stay up by myself for another hour. This is my first time alone in weeks. I notice what a strain it has been. I drink a solitary bottle of beer at the bar and then sink into the kind of bed I would like to have in America.

July 20

I wake to a wonderful day; warm but not hot. Breakfast on the terrace. All around me, many cute "fashion-kittens," some wearing bathing suits. Loewenfelds are having breakfast on their balcony. Conversation with Guenther who, much like Frede, wants to separate politics from spirit and religion. I call for M. L. who is sitting in her meadow, supremely happy. We go swimming in a blue-shimmering pool with very cold water. There are many lovely bathing beauties, including the Badoglio daughter.

Lunch with Orvieto Secco. After a nap I have coffee on the terrace, where M. L. joins me. We take a beautiful walk through the meadows while Claire and Guenther report most interestingly on Palestine. Everyone is fighting everyone else there. The capitalistic Jews in Tel Aviv, the Jewish communes (kibbutzim) which are turning Palestine with its subterranean waters into a second California; the Mohammedan Arabs who attack all Christians; the Christian Arabs who are full of hatred against the Jews; the English who always prevaricate, but finally stepped in vigorously on the side of Jewish capitalism; the Jewish proletariat, extremely powerful and dangerous. Guenther is optimistic for the Jews because the English need Jewish capitalism. Claire sees no solution: she feels that the Arabs are being treated unfairly. While in Palestine, Claire and Guenther were in constant danger of their lives. Once, the only thing that saved them was their Arab guide saying they were German Nazis. Hitler is the big man with the Arabs. Mussolini gives them money to spite the British. The Communists are severely persecuted. It is a witches' cauldron in which everything is reflected. Only Englishmen are permitted to bear arms. The Jews have founded a self-protective organization which keeps a cache of arms for emergency purposes. All the men in the settlements must do guard duty at night.

Dinner with red Capri. Long conversations, later alone with Claire, about various tensions. Claire rejects the dogmatic ties with Communism, feels unable to decide; nothing really appeals to her at the moment. Guenther's position is generally critical; he gives an excellent objective analysis.

He thinks the German economy is changing from private capitalism to state capitalism. Private capital, he says, is being eliminated through forced government loans. There is no more credit. An economic catastrophe is not to be expected, though; at best the standard of living might go down. As for international politics, he believes that Europe will fall prey to Hitler without a fight for a long time to come, until somewhere, in some unexpected place, war will break out. Without that war, he says, the United States of Europe remain unthinkable. I agree heartily with all this. Guenther travels a great deal throughout Europe, which gives him an excellent overall view.

July 21

Cloudy weather, rain; I am sitting on my balcony, writing this; have spent the entire morning writing.

Lunch with Capri. I call for M. L. and dictate to her until five. The weather clears and we go up in a cable car, which once would have been impossible for me. Wonderful walk back through a steep valley with view of the highest mountains and much new snow. There are wild strawberries in the meadows. Dinner with Frascati and Lachryma Christi. Two bad games of chess with Guenther. Beer and bed.

July 22

Waking up after sunrise, I experience a sense of dislocation, even after I get up, go to the window and see the Tofana in the red glow of morning. Not until I am on my way back to bed do I realize where I am. The sky clouds over slowly. M. L. and I go into the village to do some shopping. We have lunch while it rains. Then, despite the rain, we take the bus at two o'clock—toward Carbonin. Streaming rain on the pass. Chess game with Guenther in the hotel on the pass. Meet the nearly frozen boys of Frau Levi and Frau

Wenz, a conservative Berlin woman, tennis player, against anti-Semitism. We start out on foot from the pass hotel. The sky clears; colors and fog. Wonderful walk from the Passo Tre Croci via Lago di Misurina to Carbonin. Everywhere—especially on the Piana—there are remnants of the war to be seen: trenches, etc. The uncanny character of Carbonin. We have a wild ride back through icy cold in an open car we had ordered. I am beginning to get used to chasms.

Dinner with red Frascati. Change of clothes. Dancing. I call for M. L. who at first doesn't want to come, but then has a good time. Many beautiful Italian women. The busiest dancer is Badoglio's daughter who looks very sad. Fiftieth-birthday waltz with Claire and M. L.; on top of it all, Asti Spumante, confetti, and paper balls. I say good-by to M. L. who is being taken down by one of the men in her pensione.

July 23

I get up at six and pack, then have my last breakfast on the terrace in radiant weather. Say good-by to the children; ride down with Guenther and Claire; say good-by to Guenther and Claire. I have only just begun to feel close to Guenther. He is intelligent, very objective, and infinitely good.

Back to the Pordoi Pass by bus. Hot ride. Then over the Sella Pass with its wild vertical rock walls, into the wooded Cardone Valley; from there into the Brenner Valley, in Goethe's footsteps, to Bolzano.

Room with veranda for ten lire—two mark—seventy-five cents—in the world-famous Grifone.

Sorting the most recent letters; then a walk through the fabulous old town. A long arcade street. Many old houses, the Via Goethe. Across the Talfer. On the bridge I meet Cohnstedt and son from New York. The Promenade has a view of the Rosengarten Group, the kingdom of the dwarf-king Laurin who vanquished Dietrich von Berne. There is a wonderful violet-red evening glow on the dolomites. Dinner on the square in front of the Grifone. Red Moscato, then many mosquitoes. The place is full of German middle-class citizens.

Now I am sitting in a mosquito-free music-café, writing this. I keep looking at the lovely pictures of Erdmuthe and René, which arrived yesterday.

July 24

Up at 6:15. The sky is cloudless and a cooling wind is blowing. I have breakfast in the market square. Then a brisk ride through vineyards to Merano. Merano is hotter than Bolzano. During the ride back to Spondigna, I think over recent experiences.

I decide, despite difficulties involved, to take the detour across the Stilfser Joch. The Trafoi is beautiful but narrow. We travel along an endlessly curving road from where we see the other side of the Payer hut and the Ortler. There is not one cloud over this dazzling, petrified view. The Joch Hotel (on the highest road in Europe) is still completely engulfed in snow. At lunch I meet a gentleman from Frankfurt who had traveled with us in the beginning. To the Trilingual Peak: there are trenches, a burned-out hotel, military shelters; barbed wire marks the Italian-Swiss border. View of the Bernina. During the ride into the valley, I feel the usual fatigue. Again I go over the Ofen Pass which I had crossed in the opposite direction with Frede and Trude. Everything seems much farther away in this clear air. I have a quick cup of tea in the hotel where we had lunch that other time. Down to Zernez. One gets as used to riding alongside of chasms as to riding on trains; and one begins to feel that the human "machine," the driver, may function just as safely as a railroad engine. I spend a quiet half-hour at the Zernez station amid the fragrance of the Engadine meadows in the evening shadow of the mountains.

Up the Engadine in a little train to Bevers: the Margna,

Maloia, and Julier come into view; distance and size combine to make this, still, the most beautiful and noblest sight of all. There may be other places more convenient for Alpine tourism—but for the sheer joy of existence: give me the Engadine. Very tired, I ride to Chur, in the dark.

I go to the Hotel Steinbeck where I had taken refuge from a sudden downpour during that trip to Sils with Hannah and Erdmuthe. Local wine and prosciutto. Then to bed.

July 25

I get up at six, after a deathlike sleep. Breakfast in the garden; intoxicating fragrance of linden blossoms.

Then I leave for Zurich. The clouds are streaming with rain. To Oprecht, where I return the books. I try to locate Wendriner, finally send him a telegram; then I have a long talk with Oprecht. Serious worries over Spain. Every time I want to go to Spain, another Fascist revolution breaks out and prevents me. If the Fascists should win, the effect on France would be incalculable. Oprecht also feels that Central Europe should be ceded to Hitler: nothing is being done in Danzig; Austria is being conquered by means of quiet infiltration. Even now, anti-German books are slowly disappearing from Austrian book stores. The German part of Switzerland and German Czechoslovakia are unprotected. Swiss newspapers are pervaded by a general sense of existential anxiety.

Lunch with Bernese wine at the Hotel Simplon. At the Café Odéon I meet Hirschfeld, Wendriner, and Salome Boller. Wendriner and I take a walk along the lake. He is terribly depressed: a doctor told him a few days ago that he has a heart defect. He must live in Switzerland, at an altitude of 300 feet. He is unhappy because all the older German literature is being sold off for a few pennies; he was with Thomas Mann who, he says, is very happy and has completely freed his inner self from Germany.

Dinner with Hirschfeld. He was angry about the discussion after my lecture because Rediner insisted on questioning only my theological position, instead of discussing my sociological analysis.

We get into a big conversation about the relationship of my "order" to the Communist Party. He says: "If I were Stalin, I would ask: 'How much money do you need?' and then I would let you carry on, considering your enterprise *one* more or less successful contribution."

As I go to bed, it is pouring outside.

About my Italian experiences I must add here, which I could not do there because of the possibility that my mail might be censored, that the suppression of the Germans in South Tyrol by the Italian Fascists is disgusting: the entire population speaks German, but no German signs are permitted; all the names of towns, mountains and streets are Italianized, every wall has "Il Duce" scrawled all over it; only Italian is spoken in school, etc. Idling Fascisti lounge around everywhere, watching the Germans work. Suppression is horrifying, no matter where you encounter it.

July 26

I slept long. Today the weather is most beautiful. I am writing this on a bench by the lake, in the midst of Sunday morning atmosphere.

Departure for Berne. Lunch with the Blums on the Bellevue terrace which looks out on the Bernese Uplands. I play three games of chess with Emil Blum who is a member of the Berne chess club and has learned chess theory very well. I beat him 2 to 1.

At home, I find a lot of mail, including the most beautiful photos of the three people I love most. Also, a complicated letter from H. Schafft about his coming; and inquiry from Loewe on Stock's behalf, asking whether I would accept a teaching assignment at Manchester—philosophy of religion;

the letter from Pauck about Ann Arbor; a letter from A. Keller: my plans for Geneva have given them trouble, but now they are urgently expecting me. I unpack my trunks, then have dinner with venison and Asti. Outline of a course in education for Emil Blum. I go to bed late and am tired.

July 27

Meet E. who stays at her sister's in Berne. She has become somewhat sharp-featured, and her hair is turning gray, but she looks well. She has gone through a great deal: her family is scattered all over the world: she herself has lost her job, now lives on a small income and occasional assignments she gets from the Alliance of Christian Non-Aryans. She wants to meet her friend in Florence. He is earning the money for this trip by cutting the Olympics film for R. E. has been ill. She can no longer meet her friend, since there is no place— no matter how secluded—where there are no informers. Her worries about him have caused her a series of cardiac cramps during which she thinks she is dying; therefore, she is much preoccupied with thoughts of death. She has met the Basser- manns. He is resisting all attempts by the Nazis to get him to come home. Instead of passing on the Iffland-ring to a German actor, after Moissi's death, he donated it to the Vienna Museum, declaring that there was no more dramatic art in Germany. This has infuriated the Nazis terribly.

Before he died, Moissi asked to be placed in front of a mirror so he could act his own death and observe himself, for days on end. Bassermann, who visited him often, says it was unspeakably horrible.

E. admires the Nazis' achievements: their preparations for the Olympics; their "Winterhilfe" (winter relief action); their "Strength through Joy" program, etc. This pains her, as does her insight into the inferiority of Tucholski, for instance, whose farewell letter before his suicide was a sharp attack on the Jews—and was promptly reprinted by the

Black Corps. I try to lend her some strength by attacking the core of the Nazi system—for which she is very grateful. After we have lunch together, I leave for Fribourg.

Trude Mennicke and Woelle are at the station. It is a warm, valuable encounter. She is quite old and gray, the boy a fine figure of a fourteen-year-old. She tells me about her life: first as a teacher in the Odenwald School, then to Switzerland with Geheb, as a result of which she lost her teaching position; now her life alternates between her parents' house and that of her sister who lives in Fribourg and is married to Iserland—a newly converted Catholic. Inwardly, she is more serene than before, very critical of Karolus who had been visiting her for two weeks. She reports having a feeling of great emptiness after being with him. She confirms the "Dutch *petit bourgeois* in the making." She herself is studying Catholicism, says one needs a spiritual realm where one can feel at home, which—to her profound regret—is not possible in Marxism. I try to caution her a bit. She is a valuable person.

I wander through the magnificent ancient part of Fribourg, then leave for Geneva, where I arrive in the evening.

By car to the Pension Sergy which is a wooden house in a garden full of flowers and trees. I have dinner alone in the dining room, then to see Professor Wald; but he has already gone to bed. Some work on my lecture, then sleep.

July 28

Up at 6:45. Breakfast with Professor Wald who is a practical theologian in Strasbourg. To the Chapel of the Maccabbes in the Calvin Cathedral. There are about seventy participants. Keller gives a sermon in Barthian style. All three languages are used in the liturgy.

To the university. The first lecturer is Vischeslaszeff. He speaks on "Natural Revelation" according to the Greek Church. After every paragraph I have to translate into

English. Then a lecture by Will, in French—on culture.

Lunch with Will at the Pension. We live there as guests of the Seminar. After lunch Niebuhr appears. He has been asked to come from Stuttgart by air because the other Amercans have canceled. He is deeply preoccupied with thoughts of Germany and England. He feels that, for the moment, the danger of war has been averted. He thinks it inescapable that Germany will get everything she wants—peacefully, since none dare resist. He describes Eden as an inept functionary for Baldwin and Chamberlain. The treaty with Austria is nicknamed "The Trojan Horse." He feels that Germany is now more settled. Much rejoicing over the Olympics, little depression. In England he had a long talk with Bruening, who also admitted that the situation at the monasteries was a mess. In Holland, Bruening was in such constant danger that he had to be guarded day and night by six Dutch policemen. He will no longer set foot on the Continent. He is coming back to America.

Niebuhr had brought along the manuscript of a memorandum by the Confessing Church's synod, protesting against concentration camps, lies, rigged elections, the evil of putting children under oath, the persecution of the Jews, etc. The memorandum was read to Hitler by Schacht. In the middle of the reading, Hitler got up and walked out. Never came back. His secretary told Schacht that Hitler was taking a walk.

At four o'clock I give my first lecture; great applause, despite the fact that there are many German Nazi students present. After, Niebuhr. I have to translate him into German in minute detail, which gives me a chance to overstress his anti-Nazi points a bit. His personality makes a great impression. At the hotel I talk with Niebuhr, then have dinner with him and Will. After a stroll I go to work on my next lecture.

Breakfast with Niebuhr. To Vischeslaszeff's seminar by a roundabout road. My second seminar about America; roaring applause.

Lunch at Keller's with Niebuhr and Will. The view over the lake is beautiful. From two to four I sit by the lake with Niebuhr, each of us on a different bench, preparing our lectures. Niebuhr's second lecture, again translated by me. All very strenuous.

To the lake with Claudia Baader, H. Schafft's friend. We both complain about him. It is impossible to meet him because he cannot even decide on whether to take the trip. He has heard from Frede that I made "incautious" statements about Germany; besides, I am supposed to have said in England that the Prussian and German state was unchristian —which is, of course, balderdash when put in this form. I expressed myself much more sharply. Besides, he was told that his going to Geneva was undesirable to the church. Finally the following happened, which Keller told me: Althaus, who was on the program, asked the government whether he was permitted to speak at the same conference as the "emigrant Tillich," to which the government's answer was "no." Whereupon he declined and accepted an offer elsewhere. Keller, who was getting frightened, managed, in England—probably through the Bishop of Chichester— to make them cancel this prohibition. Nevertheless, Hermann does not dare come to Geneva now, since he is working on an auxiliary for one of the committees in Berlin. Now I hope to get him to come to Ascona; but in spite of numerous letters, no reply is forthcoming from him. Spiegelberg writes from Ascona that he has been forbidden to take part in the Eranos session. I have heard that this has happened to all German participants. The intellectuals are being more and more closely watched. Incidentally, the Spiegelbergs made an excellent impression on the Blums and Kullmanns.

Frl. Baader works at the hospital in Marburg and is very enthusiastic about von Soden. She blames Hermann for not having gone in to strengthen von Soden. She feels that H. was definitely broken by his last, unhappy love. She herself suffers greatly from Barthian orthodoxy.

In the evening there is a discussion of Niebuhr's lecture. The theological battle lines are drawn. I have to make a fairly long speech. I speak on "Politics and the Sermon." At night I work on my next lecture.

July 30

Neibuhr gives his final lecture, the best and most impressive one. He has to fly to London immediately. Before we part, we discuss a possible offer from Ann Arbor, and the definite order from Manchester which Loewe has sent me in the meantime. He says I should use both, and stay at Union, where my position is secure and "we will found a school of theology there." I have a feeling of warmth with him such as I had never experienced before.

My third lecture. Then lunch with Mr. and Mrs. Vischeslaszeff in their pension at a big family table. He is very lively, full of understanding, but not impressive.

Home to work. Then a stroll into town and dinner with Will at the pension. He asks me to come to Strasbourg next year. After dinner I go back to work and continue late into the night.

July 31

My fourth lecture. Afterward I have lunch with Maria Kullmann whose husband is in Sweden. We eat in a little French restaurant where chickens are suspended over an open grill in the dining room. Wonderful food. Delightful atmosphere. To the café on the lake. We discuss the meeting with Stepun who wants to come here. Perhaps we will arrange a little foreigners' conference in Geneva on August 20.

In the afternoon I work beside the lake. Two German students walk back with me, one of them a radical Confessing pastor in Wiesbaden. He describes the utter insecurity of the situation; he is in favor of the Free Church. Niebuhr believes that we shall have the German Free Church by winter.

Dinner with Visser 't Hooft, secretary of the World Students Christian Federation; in the *Perle du Lac* across the lake by moonlight. He is a Barthian of the reformed type. We have some very profound theological discussions. He is coming to America. At night I finish working on my final seminar.

August 1

Up at seven. My final seminar is received with tremendous, repeated applause. I am greatly relieved: it was difficult because of the German Nazi delegates, since I had to speak the truth but could not endanger the seminar.

A few hours at the Café de Genève, writing this. Schairer comes along, walks me to the International House where we had planned to dine; he and his wife; Anna Selig, and Maria Kullmann. However, Mrs. Kullmann sends her regrets. Anna Selig has great plans for Vienna. She has rented a beautiful old palace and wants to found an International House there, a kind of anti-National Socialist Austrian Cultural center. She expects great things from this and has all sorts of big ideas; she does seem to have financial backing, too. We go back to the Café with the Schairers. Later Anna Selig joins us there and, for a moment, Mrs. Kullmann puts in an appearance.

I meet three German Lutherans and we talk about the Barthian separation of the realms. It is a pleasure to have a discussion in German once again. Their mood is none too friendly toward the Nazis.

The Schairers and I go to a nice French restaurant. Good atmosphere. Afterward we walk out in the rain to see the buildings which are illuminated in honor of the Swiss National holiday. To a not so pleasant bar, where I dance one dance with Gerda Schairer. Late to bed.

August 2

A quiet Sunday morning at the pension. After lunch the members of the seminar meet for a stroll. I find myself among Polish students who speak some English and some German. They have an even harder time getting out of their country than the Germans do. The Poles want to cut them off from German culture and from the German church. Nationalism's best weapon is the scarcity of foreign exchange which in turn makes traveling almost impossible. Travel has always been the most dangerous enemy of dogmatism.

We eat in a restaurant atop a mountain ridge facing Mont Blanc which, however, we do not see since it is hidden by clouds.

I walk back with an intelligent Bavarian student. He talks of the disastrously small membership in the students' organizations, and he maintains that the student fraternities are still in existence, that the fraternity houses have not yet been taken away. The struggle continues without letup.

Sohn-Rethel appears, and we eat dinner together at his pension. He was fired just a little while ago, right after he had achieved some economic advantages for Germany in Egypt. He has a manuscript about the further development of Marxist dialectics which I am to read and give to Horkheimer. He looks miserable and ravaged. They live poorly, in the most unsuitable place, Lucerne.

We take the *Perle du Lac*, where we come upon the Schairers. Schairer and I urge Sohn-Rethel to take immediate advantage of the chance to become a French citizen. He demurs because his fifteen-year-old daughter has set her head against it.

Marvelous moonlit night over Lake Geneva. I quote: "In

such a night as this"—from *The Merchant of Venice*. Huge, illuminated fountain in Lake Geneva, taller than the highest towers. Pearls of lights along the shore. Moon over the mountains, on the water, through the trees. I return home with Sohn-Rethel.

August 3

Lilje gives a lecture; it is very good, its contents strongly derived from my own "Religious Realization." Another lecture by a Japanese Christian leader, Kagawa. A fantastic, brilliant-abstruse representation of the scale of values, and its religious versus its economic application. Very radical "Religious Socialism." I have to translate and explain the furious drawings on the blackboard. The strain is so great it almost gives me a heart attack. Afterward we have our picture taken, arm in arm.

Lunch at the Kotschnigs'. He has a very nice wife and very nice children. He is vital and good-looking, has been offered a chair at Smith College where he will be a colleague of Sommerfeld's. She, though an Englishwoman, is afraid to leave Europe. He clears up the tension between Schairer on one side and himself and Kullmann on the other. He tells me that the present High Commissioner for Emigrants is even worse than the last one was; this one keeps falling asleep at meetings. He, as Visser 't Hooft, wants Kullmann to leave the League of Nations where his talent is wasted. I have a last talk with Sohn-Rethel just before I send him to speak to Kotschnig. Later I learn that Kotschnig insisted on Sohn-Rethel's immediately applying for French citizenship.

To the university, where I meet young Seeberg and Privat-dozent Meinhold. We go to a café. The reason they've asked to see me is instantly clear to me: I am to be persuaded that things in Germany "are not really so bad"; at the same time, I am to be sounded out as to what my thinking really is. I am quite frank about my theory of the struggle between

National Socialist philosophy and religion. They insist that things are gradually easing up. For instance, they tell me that Rosenberg recently asked Erich Seeberg to come and see him, then talked to him very reasonably, almost timidly. Young Seeberg and his father regard the Confessing Church as a misfortune. The most important remark was made on the subject of war: "It is inevitable that the system receives its sanctification and sanction through force of arms . . . ."

Dinner with Visser and Lilje at the pension. Lilje reports in detail on the case "Tillich-Althaus." Althaus was asked by the "foreign minister" of the German bishop, to inquire whether he was permitted to read from the same platform as the "emigrant Tillich." Thereupon the Lutheran Council and the Confessing Church turned the case into a matter of principle. Lilje, with the consent of Maharens and the Bavarian bishop, Meiser, made it clear to the Foreign Office that an isolationist policy was nonsense. The Foreign Office agreed fully, and so did the Consul in Geneva—much to Althaus' embarrassment.

Visser and Lilje walk with me to my discussion. The "German delegation's" spokesmen are Leo Weiss.and Privatdozent Meinhold. The former tries to prove that I painted too dark a picture of the situation. In doing so, he confuses "tragic" with "bad." Meinhold defends German Lutheranism by pointing out how many important theological movements it has produced within the last few years. Some Germans and Swiss—radical Barthians—speak out with biblical pathos. In between all this, a Russian monk—the only really good speaker—takes the floor. The whole thing was poorly organized by Keller. In my final address I speak on war, the proletariat, and the English-American world, which puts the "German delegation," those from Berlin—not all the Germans present—into a bad mood, since they interpret everything from the patriotic angle. Beer with Keller, Visser, and Schairer. Mrs. Kotschnig, who had been at the meeting, too, says we are her comfort for America.

August 4

I receive a telephone call from the Blums: Hermann has difficulties over foreign exchange. I have a very late breakfast in bed. This week has practically exhausted me. I spend the rest of the morning sleeping and writing.

To the lake. Under the three fantastic trees at the pier I meet the Schairers. The lake and mountains are wonderful, as we go by steamer to the palace of Mme. de Stael, storm center of Romantic reaction against the French Revolution and Napoleon. Schairer is very passionately against the Nazis; he finds even the parallel with Communism impossible; he says that Hitler knows everything and that he is brutal and sly.

At the Schairers'—a beautiful old house belonging to the Rockefeller Foundation. Photographs. Walk to the *Perle du Lac,* where Visser 't Hooft and Lilje await me. Dinner and good wine, later the moon. Lilje is more radical than I am. He tells me that a Nazi said to him he wished for Hitler's death because that would give them "their god." We talk about various members of the Confessing Church, which he defends against Frede's criticism. He begs me to lend him Heiden's *Hitler,* which I always carry with me because I consider it the most effective book. Visser tells us about a conversation with Himmler, whom he describes as a comfortable and well-educated bourgeois. We drive to the Bavaria, where countless excellent caricatures of members of the League of Nations decorate the walls, and where a circle of students is waiting for us.

Fruitless effort to reach Hermann by telephone. Tired talk.

August 5

Hermann has to wait for foreign money. I ride to Mrs. Kullmann's. Half an hour by train. Her place is on the other side of Lake Geneva, among vineyards, fields, and parks with a view of Mont Blanc. It is a farmhouse furnished with antiques.

We eat outdoors, next to a vineyard. I ask for some wine made from these grapes, and we drink it. Deep sleep in the grass beside the vines. Coffee while Mont Blanc unveils itself. We discuss Kullmann's situation.

Back to Geneva. Frl. Baader and I talk about the theological situation in Germany during a long boat ride—wonderful colors.

Dinner at the Bavaria, and a farewell beer with the Schairers. I return early to my pension to pack my bags.

August 6

I take the train to Lausanne where I am met at the station by B., E.'s handsome brother; we visit C. who is in bed, sick, and very confused. The third friend is there, too. On the way there, B. tells me that C.'s sister has been condemned to five years in prison because of illegal activities, and that we must not talk about her. He himself, C., is slowly going to pieces because he cannot get any work.

B. and I eat together. He is doing quite well, writing short stories and crime stories; he is obviously on the way to becoming a journalist.

We are in a tall building, American style, with a café on the 14th floor and a view of Lake Geneva and the Dent du Midi.

I ride to Montreux, change over into the Alpine Railway to Les Avants, 4,000 feet above the lake, incredibly beautiful. There, at the Grand Hotel, a conference of the World Students Christian Federation is taking place under the guidance of Visser. Discussion outdoors, about a lecture by the Frenchman, Maury, on "Christian Ethics"; Piper, formerly in Münster, translates into German. I have come only for his sake. He has his family in Germany, since he does not make enough money in England. His wife is here, a very lively Jewish girl from Berlin, who looks completely Aryan. They tell me how infamously N. has behaved toward them. They blame him for Piper's dismissal, for which the party was not responsible. They tell me about their son who was being ill-treated in school because he is half-Jewish. The instigator: the son of another professor of theology.

Wonderful evening stroll up to a mountain ridge. Later I share a bottle of Burgundy with Piper, Visser, and Maury.

August 7

Up early. View of the Dent du Midi. Visser and Piper take me to the train. I ride to Montreux where I take the express train over the Simplon Pass to Domodossola—through the endlessly long, fertile Rhone Valley. I get into conversation about psychological and theological problems with a Catholic French-Swiss girl. My French comes as smoothly as ever. At Domodossola I change trains again, this time in southerly, warm, rainy weather. Through the Centovalli Valley to Locarno, the same route I once traveled in the opposite direction, playing chess with Heinrich.

In Locarno, Friedrich Spiegelberg awaits me at the station. He wears a mustache in imitation of an Indian guru, has deeply etched Indian features. Everything about him has changed greatly. He embraces me. During the ride to Ascona we have our first discussion of the situation. If he cannot find anything else, he will be allowed to go on lecturing here through the winter, though this is not really desirable since the Department of Cultural Sciences is about to be dissolved. Afterward he faces the void. His goal is to go to India.

We arrive in Ascona where a path along a wall near the post office leads up to the Villa Voltata. The Spiegelbergs live downstairs, I am upstairs with a bedroom, living room, bathroom, and a big veranda overlooking the lake in three directions. I pay 4.50 fr.—$1.50. Next door, there is another room which costs only 1.50 fr. H. Schafft is supposed to stay there. Roesli receives us with coffee. She is pretty.

We wait for a telephone call from Berne. At last, Hermann's voice on the telephone. He is coming, but he will first go to Geneva for one day, to see Claudia Baader.

We take our first walk through the town, past the Piazza, to the Lido, back to the Café Urbano, which has been somewhat enlarged; two more cafés have opened. Otherwise, everything is the way it was.

Dinner on our veranda. Phone call from Fides who has Kaete staying with her. To the Grotto garden, to meet Fides and Kaete—down near the lake, on the road to Ronco. Dancing outdoors with lights and a moon, while the lake splashes accompaniment. Delightful European-Asconese atmosphere. Fides and Kaete arrive, both in excellent shape. Kaete is quite brown and youthful-looking from her stay in Porto Fino; Fides strong and young as ever. Late to bed.

August 8

Kaete calls for us and takes us to the Lido. It is as hot as being inside an oven. Around noon the "Maloia wind" springs up. I take a solitary walk along the Lido which is quite unchanged. Many beautiful and melancholy memories. We swim in water which is not cold at all. Picnic with wine, wild frolicking in the meadows, beatific, godlike existence in joyous nature.

To the village, where everyone runs around with sandals on bare feet. Ursula von Wiese, now Frau Dr. Guggenheim, turns up. They live in Ascona. Guggenheim is a theater director, at the moment without employment. She has become heavier and calmer; there is something very maternal about her.

To Quattrino's for dinner, with Kaete. The same grape arbor, the same huge tree. Marvelous food and white Chianti.

In the evening there is a big dance at the Taverna. At a

table opposite, I see Frau Werner who still has a house in Ascona. We dance, and talk about the past. It seems that the political situation has split the people here, too. Frau Werner has turned toward the left, Frau Fritsch toward the right— and they no longer see each other. Fides seems to stand somewhere in the middle.

Much dancing and a bottle of Asti. Roesli dances with Italo, the best dancer in Ascona. Late to bed.

August 9

Working on the veranda in wonderful sunshine, while Sunday bells are ringing. Lunch at Quattrino's.

After a short nap I go to call on Frau Dr. Froebe-Kaptein, the "president" of the Eranos-Group. There I encounter some unfamiliar types: members of the high aristocracy. But first I take a swim in her garden, in the lake, near Mscha. Marvelous vegetation. A lotus flower opened just a few days ago. A Princess Mohenlohe, a Count Luettschau. I am constantly on the offensive, turning the conversation toward the fact that German professors, including Friedrich, are forbidden to participate. I speak about the need for the spirit to make a decision, and inveigh against the Group's own saint, Rudolf Otto, because he appears to have conformed to the Nazis.

Dinner on the veranda. To the Grotto where we meet a professor who explains the self-destruction of the Western powers as being caused by black magic. He is a friend of Else Lasker-Schueler's whom I had seen briefly in the afternoon. She was angry at Hugo Simon, hoarse and nervous, but looked attractive.

August 10

A telephone call in the morning announces Hermann's imminent arrival. At the same time, Frau Froebe calls to ask whether I want to speak at the Eranos. I accept; am to speak on "Salvation"—the main theme of the conference—"and the Masses."

To the Lido where I swim for fifteen minutes. Lunch at the Guggenheims'. He, very fat, with a huge shock of hair, was born in St. Gallen and knows Wolfers well. He plans to establish a traveling theater soon. They have charming children and a children's nurse. A friend from Kassel, Miss Zimmer, talks about a Spanish acquaintance who has just arrived from Barcelona. He was saved almost by a miracle and says the atrocities in Barcelona—not the Communists' but the anarchists'—are worse than the newspapers report. He, a radical anti-Fascist, would rather see the Fascists in power than these anarchist gangsters.

Hermann arrives; his face is handsome, very young and fresh. I am so glad to see him again that I simply cannot complain about all the back-and-forth of the last few days. I take him to our place; he is delighted with the view from the balcony. To the Café Centrale, where Fides arrives on her bicycle. She makes a tremendous impression on Hermann. Then Kaete, with whom a cheery conversational tone is quickly established. We—all except for the Spiegelbergs—take the bus to Heinrich's plot and climb up the famous path. Everything is as it once was. At the top, tea is served in a grape arbor. Fides' three children are there; all have wonderful faces. One of the twins, "Heinrich," resembles Heinrich strikingly. Hermann Schafft is so overwhelmed by all this beauty that he cannot say a word, later withdraws to a corner of the garden.

Fides wants to sell, and to keep only the little house at the side. With the money from the sale she wants to buy something for her brothers and sister in Germany. Dusk comes on and the lake, with Heinrich's beloved view to the south, shimmers in marvelous colors. The two women sing his songs. His purest essence is present, binding us to each other.

We eat dinner in the dark, with red Chianti. The rooms are clean and meticulously neat; there is no sign of the former dirt. We start to go. Fides gives me the ring for Erdmuthe. We descend with a lantern—it is strenuous, almost dangerous.

Kaete told me that toward the end, Heinrich had sunk more and more into a fear of black magic. At his death he felt himself pursued by hordes of gray ghosts.

We walk along the shore to the Grotto. Our melancholy mood dissolves in dancing. Fides asks me repeatedly not to forget to give Hannah her regards. She wants to be loved, not admired.

Conversations with a psychotherapist about dreams of numbers and Jung's collective unconscious.

August 11

With Hermann on the veranda, working and chatting. I dictate English letters to Friedrich. Lunch with Hermann and Kaete at Quattrino's. Deep Sleep.

Suzanne Blum comes for three days; we call for her and put her up in a nearby place. Despite some cloudiness, we go to the Lido where we swim for twenty minutes, though the water is cold. I am now back at the house, alone, sitting on the balcony, writing this; all the mountains are gray-blue.

The others return. A big dinner table is set up on my balcony: Hermann, Friedrich, myself, Kaete, Roesli, Suzanne. We have bread, ham, peaches, and Marsala. Afterward all of us, including Fides, go down to the Taverna where we meet a painter named Frick. He is a good expressionist, a fine personality, Heinrich's oldest friend among us. I watch the dancing and work on my lecture. Kaete treats us to Asti. I fall asleep deliciously by rain and wind.

August 12

Roesli and I walk to the Eranos. The weather is hot. Friedrich cannot come along because his government has forbidden it. Visheslaszeff lectures on the tragic in Europe and India. Siva-snake and Laocoön-snake.

I sit in the garden, working on my lecture while an Italian speaks.

Lunch at Frau Froebe's, who offers me her house to work in. Next to me, an old Englishwoman who knows a great deal about "Gautama" (Buddha). Frl. Pallat, the daughter of the Ministerialrat, works here as a secretary; she brings me regards from Reichwein who wants to get out of Germany.

To the Lido. A very long swim, more than twenty minutes. I make some last-minute notes for my lecture. Dinner with Friedrich, Roesli, and Suzanne; Hermann spends all day going back and forth between Ronco and Saleggio, helping Fides to move kit, caboodle, children, and maid into a tent on the lake shore; Kaete is invited to Frick's.

A large audience has assembled for my lecture. I speak with one intermission, twice three quarters of an hour. Frau Froebe is on pins and needles for fear that I might make a political gaff. I make none, though I speak very radically on politics: the idea of salvation in the present time, and Protestantism. The reaction is mixed. I learn later that the young people were all on my side, while some of the older ones felt my lecture did not belong there; and in this they were perfectly right. For what they practice there is unpolitical mysticism.

Afterward, to the Grotto where I find myself next to a handwriting expert, Pulver, who is frequently consulted by government offices. For instance, he had been asked to analyze Hitler's handwriting. He declares Hitler to be purely medial, without any personal essence of his own; and he says that Hitler will hang himself if he ever loses his medial power. After seeing a few lines of Roesli's handwriting, he knows that she has undergone an operation. He calls Friedrich an amazing recording machine, in danger of losing its self. He tells me that during my lecture, a man whom he took to be an informer had sat down next to him—and had left the hall as soon as he gave him the criminalists' secret signal. Very late to bed.

August 13

On the balcony in wonderful weather. Hermann takes Kaete to Locarno while I have a visit from Frl. Zimmer of Kassel, a friend of Ursula Guggenheim's. She asks me additional questions regarding my lecture and talks about the awful impression Hess's face made on her.

To Fides' tent at the Lido, where Hermann faithfully keeps watch. Fides and I take out a canoe. Hermann sulks on the shore. Tea in front of the tent, swimming, writing on the veranda.

Up to August 18

The Phaeacian life of Ascona, favored by magnificent weather and a soft atmosphere, blots out all memory of individual days. The general daily life is as follows: strong dislocation experiences at night, which can be mastered with the help of the phosphorescent clock face, and which point to something still to be overcome. We arise every morning in radiant sunshine. Friedrich brings breakfast—prepared by Roesli, himself, and Suzanne Blum—up to my veranda. Hermann usually visits Fides and the children at their tent. He has promised to teach the rather timid Juergen to swim. After breakfast I write letters, and make birthday preparations which are interrupted by occasional conversations. Lunch with Hermann and Suzanne at Quattrino's with a pint of white Chianti and discussions of Hermann's abstinence. Coffee on the Piazza. To the Lido to visit Fides' tent and to swim, a little longer each day if possible. Back at six. I write, the women shop for dinner: bread, butter, ham, salami, fish, fruit; and Frascati. After dinner we visit the

Grotto Chinci or the Grotto Centrale, the Taverna or the Nelly Bar. During the evenings of the Tessin folk festival, we go to the Piazza; and then, much too late, to bed.

Within this general framework, the following special events are to be noted: Thursday night in the Taverna with the wife and daughter of an antiquarian from Leipzig; though non-Aryans, they are still being tolerated by the Nazis. Fernando and Julietta, he intelligently drunk, a native of the Tessin; she elegant, German.

On Friday night at Frick's, the painter, for dinner. He has a wonderful house on the mountain, with beautiful, if not important, pictures. He knew Heinrich since 1909. He tells me about the opposition to my lecture in the Eranos by the feudal-reactionary groups. After dinner about fifteen guests arrive. Interesting discussion between the handwriting expert, Pulver, and myself. I try to extract the methodical and metaphysical elements of his specialty. He says there are three elements: the image, the flow, and the stroke. The last is the most important and cannot be imitated. Every counterfeiter can be caught by that. He uses tenfold magnification to examine a person's handwriting which is studied in three ways: through individual analysis, intuition, and radiation. There are people who are so sensitive to the radiation of handwriting that they can judge it accurately when the page is in a dark room and behind a curtain, but the curtain cannot be of silk because that cuts off the rays. Afterward there is a great discussion between Pulver—a Goethian-Freudian humanist; Friedrich—an Indian-Buddhist mystic; and myself—a Kierkegaardian Protestant. I stand alone in my intention to defend Christianity.

Sunday night with Friedrich at Frau Froebe's; conversation about "manliness" and "effeminacy" against the Nazi ideal of heroism and the "masculinization" of Christianity. Discussion about Buber.

I have many talks with Friedrich about India. He attacks

Christianity which Hermann counters with apologetic zeal. There is much tension between him and Friedrich. Friedrich considers him absurdly rigid. Hermann says Friedrich is unfair and dictatorial.

Beautiful flatboat trip with Hermann. It is touching how he looks after Fides' children. I meet him, coming out of the shrubbery, with Heinrich on his right, Marianne on his left hand—an indescribably charming picture.

I have a long talk with Frau Werner who is politically left, has helped so many refugees that she is now forbidden to take in any more lodgers, and stands in danger of being exiled. I get a report—so far unconfirmed but unfortunately all too probable—that Hirschfeld has been exiled.

Monday morning Hermann and I go on a day's excursion to the Monte Bré and the higher mountains behind it. First by bus from Locarno, up a very winding road, then on foot, without hobnails or knapsacks, carrying our lunch in a briefcase. View of Monte Rosa, the Gotthard Group, and many peaks. It is a very strenuous climb in broiling heat. We have lunch at the top. On the way up Hermann explains his objections to the Confessing Church and his reasons for working with the committees. I agree, provided he remains firm in principle. I criticize his constant use of the word "genuine," and tell him that there are no "pure cases" and that it will take a hundred years for the world to know what is "genuine" now. I do this in order to prevent him from using his hope for a "clear decision" as an excuse to avoid making any decisions of his own at all.

On the way down we keep falling on our "behind" in the tall, slippery grass. Finally my briefcase slips from my hand and rolls down a slope. We go after it, sliding on our "dignity." Hermann finds—first my fountain pen, which had jumped out, in a bush—and then the briefcase. He himself usually loses one or two of his things each day.

Coffee, wine, and a wonderful view in Monte Bré. The first drops of a gathering shower begin to fall on us. We return by bus and have dinner in Locarno, accompanied by thunder and lightning.

I help Visheslaszeff and his wife, who cannot stay in Monte Veneta now that the Eranos Conference is over, to find a place near us. I have come to know him better and find him very likable.

August 19

The eve of my birthday. Emil Blum turns up at the Café Verbanol. The others have called it off, and the Stepuns want to see me in Geneva. We go to Seewald, the painter whom we visited nine years ago when he was planning his garden. In the Great Bear exhibition his painting was the best: similar to Kanold. He shows us interesting sketches of his trip to Greece. If we want to go there, we must talk to him. He has fine brown eyes and has become a strict Catholic. His wife has a beautiful large mouth and looks as interesting as she did nine years ago. He is decorating the Pilgrims' Chapel at Ronco, near Fides' property: a wonderful job. I am happy that such things exist, and I tell him about Rivera. I walk past my steel-and-concrete house in Ronco, and past the chestnut tree by the church: the most beautiful spot on the lake. We descend through Heinrich's property and once again his spirit touches us.

While Hermann and Emil take a swim on the property, I go to visit Frau Froebe. We are quite alone, and she tells me about her exercises in concentration—every day for ten years; after about five years she began to have gnostic experiences; nowadays she can achieve concentration at will, without exercises. She herself is apolitical, rather defends my lecture, and invites us to live on her property.

Later, at the Taverna, Kaete appears unexpectedly. She had taken Ilse to the Black Forest and then simply had come back here. I go to bed dead tired after a first birthday round of clinking glasses at midnight.

I wake up at a quarter to seven. Suddenly, at seven, a four-part chorus; *"Die gueldene Sonne, der Mensch hat nichts so eigen"* ("The golden sun, man hath no good more rare"). I bawl without restraint and beg Hermann not to let anyone come in. Twenty years ago the regimental band, R.R. 72, played *Schier dreissig Jahre bist du alt"* ("Full thirty years old are you now") on the dot of seven, just like today. This is too much. And once again the people I love best are far away.

Get up. Breakfast with fifty red candles and one big yellow life-light whose streams of lava feed the smaller lights and keep them going. By and by they all burn holes into the black soil on an old serving tray which begins to look like an astronomer's map. Cake, flowers. Everyone has joined in the singing, including Fides and the Fricks. I throw them all out and read my birthday letters. The two best ones came three days ago, from Hannah and Erdmuthe.

The women are in the kitchen, preparing lunch which has been provided by the Berks and will be served in the garden of the Villa Voltata. A birthday spread with much Asti Spumante, sandwiches and fruit, beneath a pear tree. Behind the bushes, luncheon music from one of the cafés, provided by Hermann. At the table: Hermann, Fides, the Spiegelbergs, Frick and Frau Fellinger, the Visheslaszeffs, the Blums, Kaete, Frau Dr. Rumpf who happened to stop by here on her way to Pallenza. The atmosphere is charming. Hermann and Frau Fellinger take lots of photographs.

General nap time. Then coffee, and off to the lake by motorboat. We have a great swim in indescribable water. At six everyone assembles on my balcony for a discussion. Subject: the idea of progress. I initiate the discussion from the American viewpoint. Speeches by Frick, Hermann, Emil, and, best of all, Visheslaszeff. Frick has given me a sketch suggesting Ascona. It is very beautifully executed. We feel a profound liking for each other. The postman brings the folder with tributes from various friends. "That is Hannah's work." Thank you, my dearest!

Great dinner table at Quattrino's. The best *vino nostrano, pollo amato;* after dinner, renewed discussion. I come out too vehemently against Hermann.

We dance at the Taverna. I go to bed very late, and very much moved by torrents of love. Telegram from Loewe and Staudinger.

August 21

I wake up, a man of fifty, Kaete and Dr. Rumpf depart. I take a last swim in indescribable water. Then I visit Dr. Heilbrunn (not Heilbrunner). He knows me from Hiddensee and Frankfurt. He sees Europe as I do and is very perceptive. Farewell gathering at the Grotto Chindi. Fides wants to leave while I am dancing. But I tell her that we must not become sentimental. We have found each other in Heinrich's memory—and only in that. For the rest, I find her strange and admirable.

Back to Ascona in Frl. Pallat's canoe. Very late to bed.

August 22

Up very early. At 8:00 the trunks are picked up. At 8:30 I say good-by to Hermann, which is very hard, just as it was during the war. At 9:30 I say good-by to the Fricks, the Blums, and the Spiegelbergs—all framed by the window of a bus; I look at their faces as if it were for the last time. Half an hour earlier I had dictated a letter to Friedrich asking Oldham to help Friedrich get to India. Friedrich was the most mature person there: he has become an Indian.

On August 19 he had given my handwriting to Pulver. The verdict was shattering: ambivalence between richly developed instinctual life and built-up intellectual development. Lack in the dimension of the soul, symptoms of dissolution threatening psychophysical catastrophe. Some errors there, but most of it is correct. Ascona was a profound analytical move into the past for me.

I forgot to mention a charming birthday telegram from Else Lasker-Schueler: "To the 15-year-old or 50-year-old."

I have great difficulty in tearing myself away, but in the last analysis I am quite glad to leave. The train goes through Centovalli which I experience more intensely than ever before. Across the Simplon, through the Rhone Valley, to Montingy. Then, in the Alpine train, to Chamonix. I am very tired. It is cloudy. The Hotel Stadtgang is very big and chic. The glaciers of the Mont Blanc Range almost reach all the way down here. I am writing this at the Music Café, while it rains outside. I go to bed, reeling with fatigue, and have ten hours of deep sleep.

August 23

I wake up in Chamonix to sunshine and fog. Breakfast in bed, after which I take care of my mail, the watch, and some other errands. In sunny-cloudy weather, I ride up to Mont Anvers, the chief starting point of all Alpine tours, complete with hotel. I spend an hour on the glacier: Mer de Glace. If you have no nails on your shoes you can buy socks here for walking on the ice—but my white shoes are all right. Lunch at the hotel, then a long walk beneath stone fields and glaciers, across the Chamonix Valley to Plan des Aiguilles. Clouds shroud the peaks which become visible for a few moments only. Magnificent, especially the Aiguille de Dru. I have coffee at the Plan House.

To the Lac des Nantemilles, where I am haunted by persistent memories of the Lies Grischus—Hanno Gelau experiences.

I fight down the temptation to walk across Le Glacier des Pélègrins to the Station des Glaciers. For two hours I descend at a furious pace through dark woods. Dinner and coffee at Chamonix. Deep sleep. I dream of having to seek a warrant for my arrest at the Gestapo, not finding it, and deciding to flee.

August 24

As I get up, the sun begins to break through the prevailing haze. To the post office, where I meet Dr. Metzger and Frau Klausner-Levi, the nice woman who came to see us in New York. She is now married to Metzger, is charming and happy —he seems much better than before. We sit in the café until eleven o'clock. He talks about the Philosophers' Congress that is to take place in Paris in 1937; he wants to get me invited to it. He is professor at the Jewish School in Berlin. She would like him to go to Paris where he has a chance of obtaining French citizenship. I urge him to listen to her. He wants to climb Mont Blanc the day after tomorrow and asks me to come with him. I decline, weeping silently.

He tells me about Veronika Czapski who has written some excellent new poems but whose basic development is hampered, he says, by her marriage and bourgeois surroundings.

I take the cable car up the side facing Mont Blanc, then walk the main road to Mont Bervent on foot, to save money. Climbing up a crevasse with my briefcase and in my white shoes. At the top, the most wonderful panorama presents itself: the Mont Blanc Range, the Bernese Uplands, the Dauphiné. Two hours to Point Flechers—from where the view is more toward the Aiguille du Dru. The mountains are red and getting redder in the evening sun. Ecstasy of beauty. An idea for an address on beauty for American audiences occurs to me.

Down through the woods with glimpses of the red-glowing mountains. The glow fades from the 9,000-ft. and the 12,000-ft. peaks. Mont Blanc remains alone, the grandest of mountains. Then Mont Blanc, too, lies in darkness. There remains the moon—the heavenly body. Ivory whiteness of the glacier. I walk back along a steaming brook.

While having dinner and coffee I am barely able to move my arms or legs.

August 25

Up early to pack my bags. As the train goes along the Chamonix Valley, the view of the sun-baked Mont Blanc Range changes continually. The southwesterly peaks of Mont Blanc come into view.

At St. Gervais les Bains I change trains and continue along a wide valley with big hotels and wonderful distant view of Mont Blanc.

Through La Roche to Genève-Eaux-Vives. Schairer is at the station. We have lunch at the Régence. He is, as always, full of stories about the political situation. For instance, he tells me that Geldte has threatened that all Genevans will be sent to concentration camps when the Germans march into Switzerland. Kullmann calls for us in his car, and we race out to Céligny. Natascha appears; her face is unchanged, but she has grown much fatter, especially around the hips. Then Stepun, whose hair is now completely silver-white. They give me a very warm welcome.

My first talks with Stepun are about people. He describes Ida Bienert as all temperament. She lives very withdrawn, spends very little time in Dresden; her pictures are unchanged, but she won't let anyone see them. The rest of the faculty has been dispersed. The teachers' training program is in the pedagogic academy, Stepun in the department of economics, with four students and many unmatriculated listeners. The best is the historian Kuehn who speaks very openly against the regime. Stepun has social contact with Nazis and enjoys pulling the Gestapo's leg. He feels that the Nazis are the framework within which it is still possible to work, refuses to attack the regime as such. I report on the

European situation and on Hitler's victory on the Continent. He is deeply shaken, feels that he has taken Nazism too lightly.

During dinner, outdoors, we have further basic discussions about the world situation, religion, and Communism. Kullmann and I are in complete agreement. We drive Schairer to the train. The Stepuns and I have rooms in the old tower; their room is above mine. These are circular rooms with terribly thick walls. Vine leaves and mosquito nets add to the very romantic atmosphere.

August 26

I wake up to the sounds of Russian songs—sung by Stepun. We have coffee outdoors, followed by a morning discussion about Wolfers' birthday contribution in which he discusses the Church and Communism. We agree on many things.

The morning paper carries the news that Stalin has had his former comrades-in-arms shot. A shattering revelation.

After lunch Kullmann and I go into town. Wally Schulz and Emmerich await us at the Café de la Régence. Wally is very youthful, has bicycled all the way here from Frankfurt. She tells me about everyone I know. Their main social contacts are the Reinhards. The Florsheims have got out, after his passport had been temporarily confiscated. Platzhof is dull and not very happy. There is a ubiquitous system of spies and informers, but one gradually becomes used to the pressure. The separation of Jews and Aryans is being more and more taken for granted. Wally would like to get out. Peter wants to be retired, since he can no longer bear to watch the destruction of the university. Reinhard is very cautiously influencing his students. The Hoechbergs are waiting for permission to emigrate.

Back to Céligny with Schairer and Kullmann. We have discussions by the fireplace which we continue, later, in our circular tower rooms. Religious discussions and questions with me. At the park wall, under the stars. Russian-mystical atmosphere.

August 27

In our final discussion, in the garden, we talk about the future of the Church and of Protestantism, and about the idea of a league, or order.

In the afternoon the Kullmanns take me into town where I meet Schairer at Lake Geneva. We talk about the youth conference in which he participates. Youth without leadership.

I make preparations to leave Switzerland. Hotel in town. View of Mont Blanc from above. I begin to rearrange my luggage for the trip back.

An autumnal haze lies over the lake. I go to bed early. Kullmann and Maria have suggested we say "thou" to each other.

August 28

Farewell ride up Mont-Salève which lies near Geneva but across the French border. Three thousand feet by cable car. All the peaks, Mont Blanc and all its promontories are visible above an ocean of haze in a delicately blue sky. Indescribable beauty. Gradually, the haze dissolves. City and lake emerge.

I have lunch at the top and return quite late to continue laboring over my luggage. Then I meet the Kullmanns at the Café Régence. They take me to Céligny by car. It is my farewell evening with them and the Stepuns. Chianti and phonograph records: Russian, French, Hungarian, Italian. The atmosphere is very beautiful and not at all abstract. Everyone is incredibly warm and cordial. Russian mysticism is in its vital sphere here. Afterward everyone comes along to take me to the station and we have an emotional leave-taking, filled with a profound sense of fate. Stepun wants to get out as soon as he can; but it is very hard for him. I walk back to my hotel along Lake Geneva, under a starry sky.

August 29

I get up early and spend the entire morning packing. The big trunks are ready to be shipped. The Kullmanns and Stepuns come to take me for a farewell lunch. At the Restaurant Globe with a wine called Vignes de Notre Seigneur. Stepun, the *bon vivant*. Final parting at the railroad station.

At the passport inspection in Bellegarde I am suspected of being a German spy against France because my route takes me through Luxembourg, where I hope to meet Margot and, perhaps, Reinhard. I am not allowed to get off the train at Sedan, Charleville, Reims. Signs of European tension. It is a long, hot train ride through a landscape that looks like one big garden, toward Dijon. I forgot to mention that on my last evening, from the Kullmanns' place, I had a very affectionate telephone conversation with my father. Very moving farewell speeches over the telephone.

The Côte-d'Or comes into view; here is where Burgundy grapes are grown. Arrived in Dijon, I send my luggage straight through to Paris; then I go to the Hotel Central, feeling somewhat uneasy because of what happened at the border, and because of the situation in general.

August 30

I wake up—to a blindingly bright Sunday morning—after several moments of uncertainty during which I think that I am on top of a high mountain.

Sightseeing in this city, the former capital of Burgundy, is very rewarding. There are three main churches in the original Burgundian style; there is the palace of the Dukes of Burgundy, and there are many amazing private houses, all in the richest of Renaissance styles: this is truly an old princely residence. I have a fantastic dinner, which includes white Burgundy, within view of the palace.

I continue on to Luxembourg, which is an eight-hour ride with five train changes. Add to this that it is Sunday afternoon and very hot. The landscape is very German and close to my heart.

Toward evening we reach the wartime region near Metz. At the Metz railroad station I reexperience the air-raid alarms of the time when I was on leave from the army—then we pass through Pont-à-Mousson, Longuyon, etc. Many of my fellow passengers are soldiers in fantastic red uniforms. The moon emerges from between small white cumulus clouds.

I arrive punctually in Luxembourg and find a room at the Hotel Alpha. Dinner with Luxembourg Moselle at eleven o'clock. It is nice to be able to drink Moselle with a good conscience and without breaking the boycott. The atmosphere has become noticeably German from Metz on: German soldiers' songs on the train, German folk songs at the café, played by an all-girl band; a German moon—and a German landscape; but the official language, fortunately, is French.

At the café a gentleman starts up a conversation with me. In rather peculiar German he insists he has been to Africa and assures me that "order and discipline" reign in Germany, and that Communism cannot possibly win, etc. Though I do not react to any of this, he shakes my hand most cordially when saying good-bye; wants to see me again—I don't. Deep sleep after that strenuous trip.

August 31

I write letters till noon, then call for Margot Faust. At first we miss each other in the milling crowds at the station —the Luxembourg *kermesse*. Then we meet at the hotel. Margot has aged gently and her hair is now gray; but otherwise she is as strong and tart as ever. At lunch we begin to talk, warming up slowly. She lives in Lübeck, totally alone, has no circle of friends or acquaintances. She reads voraciously, in winter up to six hours a day. She does have a steady friend in Saarbrücken whom she sees at least once a month; she also sees Erich. Erich is a big wheel, a member of a board of directors. He has a big garden which is taken care of by gardeners from the factory; also, a private car and an official car. He wants to move, preferably to Essen, perhaps as a director for Krupp.

We stroll through town, which is jammed with people from the country. All the shops are selling all their rubbish, outdoors.

We sit down in an old square with autumnal chestnut trees. Slowly, we get around to the subject of politics. Result: Erich and Margot are inwardly firm, nor do they make any outward concessions. They can afford this, since they are both popular and socially respected. In her view of the Nazis, Margot differentiates between cultural and social developments on the one hand, and achievements in organization and public works on the other. She approves of the latter, as almost everyone does, but rejects the former. She stanchly opposes the intrusion of the total state into education and other private spheres. She considers herself a liberal, and, as such, she also rejects the racial system, though she prefers it, in principle, to the Fascist system. There seems no doubt that the upper stratum of the working class has been integrated into the system and feels its situation has improved; nor, that the economy has been revitalized, even without rearmament activities. Also, that a number of individual edicts have dictatorially eliminated certain evils. One very clever move is being planned: some reliable "neutrals" are to be called into the party and to be given equivalent rank with those who carry party numbers below 100,000. Erich is among those who are being considered. Margot is very much against the resurgent militaristic ideology. Every boy wants to become an army officer, and the active officers are as overbearing as ever. A similar spirit makes itself felt everywhere. The other day Markus was beaten in school by the teacher. He, like Buzi before him, is to be sent to the Odenwald School, which is still tops.

At 6:30 Mr. Brasseur calls for us in his car. He is a Luxembourg iron merchant with a fabulous country estate. Very nice; he has a rather Dutch sense of humor. His wife is a pretty, somewhat vapid Rhenish type. We walk through the terraced park with its long flower beds and its view over valley and woods. The house is a beautifully remodeled monastery, furnished in the French style. For dinner there is a wonderful Moselle. Agricultural conversation about a biologico-dynamic fertilizer system which Steiner invented and which is said to be excellent. Struggle against chemical fertilizers. Interest in American literature. Very pleasant atmosphere. On our way back, in his car, we stop to see the view from the highest part of town into the valley that surrounds Luxembourg like a huge moat. Margot and I continue our conversations at a café. She is very versatile and vivacious. At the end of the day I am dead tired.

September 1

Reinhardt, who is supposed to come from Amersfoort, sends me a telegram to say he cannot come because of "technical" difficulties. I am very sad.

I go sightseeing in the old part of town. There are many ancient streets but few antiquities. Wonderful are the surrounding walls of rock and the deep valleys beyond. Lunch at the old Restaurant Cravate; excellent French food.

After a short rest I get ready to move on tomorrow. Margot and I take a long walk into the surrounding countryside. Margot is afraid of dogs, just like Hannah. Stubble fields, autumnal haze, autumn flowers. I am deeply drawn into the autumnal atmosphere. Dinner at Cravate with Burgundy. I explain my ideas systematically.

Up at 6:30—I leave for Paris. It is a hazy autumn morning. The train follows my old wartime furlough route, Longuyon-Sedan; today is Sedan Day in the old Germany. The sun breaks through the clouds: this wonderful autumn day reminds me of maneuvers of old. It gets warmer and warmer. We pass Mezieres-Charleville, where I often went when it was the German headquarters, and where Captain Pfeiffer discovered his Suzanne. Challerange, where the switchyard for the Reims front used to be; Rethel, the first stopping place, Bézancourt, where one of our regiments was stationed; Vity les Reims, of which I have particularly horrible memories; Reims itself with its cold-looking renovated cathedral; in between, artillery emplacements, trenches, soldiers. Cemeteries. Near Meuse, a monument to the battle of the Marne. Heavenly Marne landscape! We enter Paris. I go to my old hotel where lots of mail awaits me.

Preparing the homeward journey is hard labor. I go to the French Line, to the Gare St. Lazare and to the Gare de Lyon. I also spend an hour at the Tuileries, writing a letter to Loewe. Countless brilliant late summer flowers glow under the evening sun. The Louvre is visible in the background—this is my quietest, most beautiful hour in weeks.

After dinner at good old Delpuech's I ride to Montparnasse and stroll through the streets where Eckhart and I had said good-bye. The moon is out. There are crowds at the Café Coupole.

I visit the bar of the Monocle, which is a rather done-up night club with a floor show.

September 3

I have tea in bed, take a bath, write some letters. At the Sainte Chapelle the windows are easier to see and as beautiful as those at Chartres.

La Conciergerie, the prison of the Revolution and the September murders: Marie Antoinette shall stoop (bend down) when led to her cell; for this purpose, a small opening is cut out of the tall door and the rest is nailed shut. Compare today's revolutions!

Inside Notre Dame: more beautiful and clearer than I had remembered it. I walk past Notre Dame on the opposite shore and back through old streets to St. Michel. Lunch at Steingart's, our favorite place ten years ago. Very good, but expensive.

Ancient streets near St. Jacques le Pauvre. The bookstalls on the bank of the Seine. I stop at a café in the rue Rivoli, then walk through the Palais Royal. I also buy a new hat and a few other things.

There is a continuous exchange of air mail letters between Loewe and me. England now seems uncertain.

In the evening I have a good dinner on Montmartre, then look in on the Tabarin and on some tourist places, but find them very unsatisfactory. Thus I get to bed by one o'clock.

September 4

After writing some letters, I go to the Louvre where I repeat the routine of my last visit. Everything here is nearly smothered by its own sheer quantity. Only the very greatest works stand out. The way things are hung in the *grand galerie* is basically barbarous; it reminds me of the Palazzo Pitti.

In the morning, just as I finish my tea in bed, Professor Marti of Oberlin appears and talks to me about Spiegelberg's chances in America.

For lunch I meet Mr. H. Sahl, Emmy Sach's friend, the "typical" intellectual immigrant; terribly starved, delighted with the Vouvray at Delpuech's. He tells the fantastic story of George Bernhard and the rape of the Paris daily. He also says that the Communists support corruption, all because of the Front Populaire. He declares that he has been pushed aside because of this struggle against corruption among emigrants; he wants to go to America. While he tells me all this, his chief opponent keeps walking past our café. Sahl also talks of *Rollkommandos* (vigilantes) among the emigrants. It sounds ghastly.

Afterward I take a nap, then go shopping. In the evening I have dinner near the Porte St. Martin. Later I walk to the empty quarter of Montparnasse. From there through the Halles. I sit down in a café where a slightly demented, totally ragged and filthy old Jew begs for bread and wine with great dignity. In front of the café, mountains of cabbage and cauliflower are piled up into pyramids. The cabbage is very fragrant.

I overhear a political discussion between an intellectual leftist and a self-assured rightist, at a table nearby. The rightest is a much better speaker, but not likable.

All the streets are full of cabbage and fruit. Fantastic mountains of red radishes.

September 5 and 6

Adolf telephones from England to say I absolutely must come because of Manchester. He had planned to come to Paris to visit with Hilde Oppenheimer, who has now been Frau Dr. Blum for the last two months. This might have saved me the trip to England. I accept his invitation, then spend the morning and afternoon getting my tickets and taking care of my luggage. Lunch near the Madeleine. At 5:00 P.M. I leave from St. Lazare for Le Havre, via Rouen.

The weather gets rougher. Wind and rain squalls. In Le Havre, by taxi to the ship for England. I check my luggage in a gloomy harbor street, then walk to the harbor, right up to the water's edge, in darkness, storm, and rain. At the ship's starting point the streets are full of bordellos; in every hallway stands a fat old madam, calling you in. Instead, I go on board and am somewhat appalled by the smallness of the ship. I had thought at first that this was the tender that would take us to the ship itself.There are only two classes: first and second. Second class is like the oldtime steerage: a single room with tiered bunks for about forty men. I spend the hour before the ship sails on deck, looking out at the harbor lights and at the ships of Le Havre and—on the other side—the lights from Trouville and Deauville of happy memory. The waves in the harbor get bigger, our ship begins to roll. We pull away from the Continent; red and green lights. I take a Vasano pill, but, foolishly, after a glass of beer. Therefore, the pill has no effect. After half an hour I begin to be seasick. It lasts almost four hours and is more horrible than anything I have so far experienced in this respect. The ship dances and, at every turn, my insides erupt until the last drop of bitterness is spilled. Some others in the room are somewhat better off than I, but the majority are much worse. At five o'clock I catch an hour's sleep in the Channel after Southampton. Then up for passport inspection and luggage.

To the railroad station to catch a train to Bournemouth. I interpret for a French lady. As we have to wait for almost two hours for the next train, I go to the nearest hotel to freshen up and have some breakfast. The stomach accepts tea and buttered bread.

Long train ride along the southern coast; change of trains, then a cross-country taxi ride. Shortly before Toller I meet Adolf and the youngest child. We go to their house together.

Lunch and a long nap. During an extended walk with Adolf, I speak without any voice; the terrible retching has strained my throat.

Wonderful, wavy green landscape; in the background lies the sea. We discuss the Manchester offer in detail, also in respect to the general world situation and in view of our task. We also go very thoroughly into the financial aspect of the proposal. We return in the rain and have dinner;

talk about some of Adolf's work and works. About Peter's book which has led to conflict between him and both of us, which he takes personally in my case. Very tired, I go to bed, while the storm rages outside. With a compress over my throat, I find ten hours of the deepest kind of sleep.

September 7

Sunshine and a northwesterly wind. Continued, very detailed conversations with Adolf. We talk about the problem of personal sacrifices, while wandering up a hill. There is a cornfield and a view over many hills, to the sea. Lunch.

The Stocks call for us in a car and drive us through the green Dorset countryside. We walk up a hill with a pre-Roman settlement characterized by high earthworks. Wonderful view of sea and hills.

The Stocks' house in West Bay lies directly at the outlet of a little harbor into the sea. Northwesterly storm and high waves, although it is low tide. The shores are steeply eroded by the sea.

We talk about Manchester. He offers me a lectureship with £500—not as he had originally told Adolf, a readership, which goes up to £750. Three to four hours a week, more than five months' vacation, no pension; compulsory insurance. The connection with other universities would be difficult, but not impossible. He feels himself that this offer is inadequate, saying that he is suggesting to a "whale" what would be suitable for a "trout." His best argument is the beauty of the English countryside and the small work load. After we get back, Adolf and I decide we must hold out for the readership.

A wonderful telegram from Hannah came half an hour before the Stocks' arrival.

The colors of the landscape are lovely; not so harsh as the autumn colors in America. After dinner we talk very comfortably by the light of petroleum lamps.

September 8 and 9

I have spent two great days with Loewe. Morning and afternoon walks in the green hillscape; along paths flanked by walls of greenery; blackberries; wide vistas; autumnal haze. I get up late, and go to bed late. We drink cider instead of wine. We celebrate Rahel's birthday, visit an old farmhouse, use petroleum lamps and candles. There is an old cemetery with the graves of members of the Churchill family.

We talk in the mornings and afternoons during our walks. The second day we wander through fog to the pre-Roman settlement. Brambles, cows, sheep. Subject of our conversation, the dialectics of National Socialism in the aspect of the four stages: swampy meadow, hill, sea, high mountain range. (1) The present; (2) the immediate future; (3) the aimed-for-future; (4) the distant future. We must work toward (1) by overcoming (2) dialectically. The problem of dictatorship, even a dictatorship of our own. The idea of the democratic corrective. Discussions about religion, the super-id and the super-thou. The third stage in the sense of Joachim of Floris and Heinrich. The tasks: for Adolf—the politico-economic aspect; for me—the "dogmatics." General problems related to the Manchester problem. The path of "emptying out." Deepest community with Adolf. Review of friends.

September 10

Off to London after a telephone call to Oldham. On the train I get into conversation with a nice young Englishwoman. Mr. and Mrs. Oldham call for me and take me to lunch at the hotel. He is grealy excited about Manchester, insists that I accept nothing less than a readership. Then there would be further possibilities. We discuss the ecumenical situation; I report on the talks I have had with Loewe. He is delighted and says he would like to make me the director of Oxford in 1937. He wants to co-opt me for this purpose. His wife drives me to Waterloo Station.

I take the train to Portsmouth and from there a ferry to Ryde on the Isle of Wight. Julia is waiting for me at the bridge. We drive to Bimstead. They are living on an old country estate in a wild, unkempt park with incredible trees on the Watt side of the island. All the big ships pass by there. The *Europa* lay at anchor right in front of their house; next day the *Lafayette* was there, too.

Mannheim is in bed with a slight cold. My report on my travels in Europe moves them deeply because they feel farther from Europe, in England, than we do in America. They—especially Karl—reject England and criticize Adolf's article about English conformity. Dinner at the pension. Conversaion at Karl's bedside. Sherry, and deep sleep.

September 11

I have breakfast with a doe-eyed English medical student. Beautiful walk through the island to an old fishing place. The inflexibility of English conformity. I have my last lunch in Europe, then by bus across the island. I say good-by to the Mannheims: this is my last good-by.

Across to Southampton and down to the pier with my luggage. I stroll through the very beautiful old town, admire the magnificent town gate, the town walls, and some old warehouses.

Returned to the pier, I spend several hours on the tender. Sunset over the harbor. The train from London arrives, and I strike up an acquaintaince with a Miss Nix-James, a professor of educational psychology—a mixture of schoolteacherish and lively. She knows about me from Woodbrook where there was much talk about my lecure. She also knows Heinrich Becker. We cross to the ship in the dark, which takes almost an hour and a half; then we go on board. Dinner is served around 11:00 P.M. Having located all my luggage, I find I am housed in a large stateroom with two other passengers. After some time up on deck, I have a good night, what with the artificial ventilation in the stateroom and neighbors who do not snore. The ship rocks gently, I am glad that my wanderings are over.

September 12

I am the first one up. After breakfast—with cornflakes—I take a deck chair. There is a broad groundswell and such a dense fog that the ship is occasionally forced to a complete standstill. Then warm sunshine replaces the fog. I begin to read manuscripts. Lunch with Miss Nix-James and two American professors: Professor Hall, a historian, who is a close friend of Niebuhr's and who knows my book; and Professor Aksin, a political economist in Boston. We immediately plunge into interesting talk. Hall has spent three weeks in Germany with his two daughters, has visited twenty-seven youth camps, and says that, although he likes the German people more than any other Europeans, he came back literally ill because of their ideology: militaristic, anti-Semitic, anti-Negro, unchristian, adoration of Hitler. Aksin is afraid of American Fascism.

After lunch I sleep deeply for two hours. Wonderful blue ocean. Before dinner I take a stroll through the first class. A chess game with the English miss. Watching the dancing. The autumnal sky is full of stars.

September 13

I am the second one up. Conversations with a student of Morris Cohn and with Professor Hall. The sky is blue, and it is windy. Sunday. I am reading the birthday manuscripts. A northwest wind springs up and brings some showers. At noon and in the evening I talk with the two professors. One of my cabin mates is the Swiss Vice-Consul in Mexico. He

talks very interestingly about the impossibility of civilizing that country and about the corruption of the government which helps to make the task of settlement impossible.

In the evening, chess with Miss Nix-James. Dance on the enclosed deck, which is not very attractive.

September 14

As I wake up the ship rolls heavily, and I reach for the Vasano. Soft, rainy weather. I spend the morning writing, sorting letters and photographs. At lunch and dinner the two professors do not seem to feel too well. I spend the afternoon on deck in soft, moist weather.

In the evening—four games of chess with a German businessman. I meet Brauer who was the mayor of Altona once and later lived in China and New York. I go to bed with the usual glass of vermouth.

September 15

Streaming rain—and the ship rolls. Vasano. I work in the writing room. Northwest weather. The waves and ·vind increase. It is very cold.

I continue reading manuscripts. After lunch I spend a long time in bed. Between 4:00 and 6:00 p.m. I see countless rainbows, fantastic colors, huge waves. I feel slightly indisposed.

Dinner, then chess. I win one game, another ends in a draw. Early to bed. The ship rolls heavily. Sleep.

During lunch I had a conversation with Professor Aksin about the League of Nations and the possibility of power organization. He, too, is very skeptical.

September 16

Blue sky and a slight wind; it's very cold. I read and write letters on deck. Clouds and rain. I withdraw to the writing room. The sky clears and it gets very cold. To the north of us there is an iceberg. It looks like a little glass tower, a white-greenish mass to the naked eye. I spend some time filling out customs forms.

Dinner with sauterne and lively talk. Professor Aksin has presided over the Jewish New Year's celebration; he tells us about Jewish rites. He speaks Hebrew and Yiddish.

Chess. I win one game, lose two. Early to bed. Dislocation anxiety.

September 17

Autumnal spring weather. I feel tremendously relaxed and too lazy to work. Everyone is up on deck. At breakfast, conversation with a French-American schoolteacher; she is afraid of Hitler.

On deck I talk with an Englishwoman who is married to a Negro and seems to be very happy with him. They want to come and see us.

At night there is a big gala dinner with Vouvray *sec mousseux*. Afterward, a floor show by the guests, not very interesting.

Chess, until the chessmen are overturned by a cannonade of cotton balls. Moist warm air. In the afternoon I had a talk with a nice lively French girl who is to spend a year at an American college, teaching French sixteenth-century literature; she wonders how she will interpret Rabelais to the Americans. I also talked with a Spanish-American girl who had just spent three months in Barcelona and says all is quiet there now. She is passionately anti-Fascist, tells me about her brothers who are in the opposite camp.

September 18

Up early. The weather is hazy, which later turns to fog. Packing, more letters and some post cards to write. Good table talk about the American concept of Experience. Sleep. I write some last-minute letters and send a radiogram to Hannah.

The ground swell gets stronger. Reports of an approaching storm. At first there is fog, then rain. The sea looks uncanny and magnificent. At dinner everything is clamped down. I am not very hungry.

Victorious at chess, also against Brauer. I go to bed at 11:30.

The ship rolls more violently than it did during the entire trip so far. The storm breaks; it is the tail end of the Bermuda hurricane. The ship rolls furiously and spray comes in through the porthole. Then the ship lies motionless for several hours, which produces an uncanny feeling. I get very little sleep.

September 19

I get up early to do my final packing. The weather is calm. Long Island comes into view. We arrive.

Notes to Introduction

1. Paul Tillich, *The Interpretation of History*, 1936, pp. 3 ff. Reprinted under the title, *On the Boundary* (New York: Charles Scribner's Sons, 1966).
2. Paul Tillich, *My Search for Absolutes* (New York: Simon and Schuster, 1967), p. 50.
3. Paul Tillich, *My Travel Diary: 1936* (New York: Harper & Row, 1970), p. 38.
4. *Ibid.*, p. 42.
5. *Ibid.*, p. 56.
6. *Ibid.*, p. 76.
7. *Ibid.*, p. 120.
8. *Ibid.*, p. 174.
9. Tillich, *Interpretation of History*, p. 68.
10. *Ibid.*, pp. 41 f.
11. Paul Tillich, *Christianity and the Encounter of the World Religions* (New York: Columbia University Press, 1963), pp. 29 ff.
12. Tillich, *My Search for Absolutes*, pp. 26 f.
13. *Ibid.*, p. 25.
14. Tillich, *Interpretation of History*, p. 7.
15. *Ibid.*, p. 8.
16. Tillich, *My Travel Diary*, pp. 100-101.
17. Paul Tillich, *The Religious Situation* (New York: Meridian Books, 1956), p. 85.
18. Tillich, *Interpretation of History*, p. 14.
19. Tillich, *Religious Situation*, p. 89.
20. Tillich, *My Travel Diary*, p. 108.
21. *Ibid.*, p. 81.
22. Tillich, *My Seach for Absolutes*, pp. 45 ff.
23. *Ibid.*, p. 45.
24. Mircea Eliade, "Paul Tillich and the History of Religions," in Paul Tillich, *The Future of Religions*, ed. by Jerald C. Brauer (New York: Harper & Row, 1966), p. 33.
25. Tillich, *My Search for Absolutes*, p. 54.
26. Tillich, *Interpretation of History*, p. 18.

Glossary of Names

The purpose of this glossary of names is simple. It aims to identify only close friends of Tillich or persons of public significance. In some cases the context in the diary provides necessary information. Not all names can or need be explained. In no case is there an attempt at definitive identification; rather, a statement is provided so the reader will have some idea of the person to whom Tillich refers. Identifications are listed in the order as the names appear on particular pages.

Page 27

HANNAH AND ERDMUTHE are the wife and daughter respectively of Paul Tillich. Their names appear frequently throughout the diary. The Tillichs' infant son René is also mentioned several times. As Tillich wrote the pages of the diary he mailed them home in secitons to his wife Hannah and so kept her posted on the trip.

HANS SIMON is a distinguished German emigre to the United States who became Head of the New School for Social Research in New York. In prewar Germany he was a provincial governor. Since his retirement from the New School, he has had a third career with the Ford Foundation.

DR. KURT GOLDSTEIN was a famous neurologist and psychiatrist, one of Tillich's closest friends and a fellow emigree.

PROFESSOR MAX HORKHEIMER was a personal friend of Tillich and former director of the Institute for Social Research at Frankfurt, at which university he was a colleague of Tillich. After fleeing Germany, Horkheimer taught in the United States, returning after the war to the University of Frankfurt.

Page 31

EDUARD HEIMANN, an *émigré* friend of Tillich, became Professor of Political Economics at the New School for Social Research in New York. In the late 1950's he returned to Germany and taught at the University of Hamburg. Heimann was a frequent lecturer at Union Theological Seminary and belonged to the Fellowship of Socialist Christians.

Page 34

MRS. URSULA NIEBUHR is the wife of Professor Reinhold Niebuhr, world famous theologian who was instrumental in bringing Tillich to the United States where they became colleagues and close friends at Union Theological Seminary, New York. Mrs. Niebuhr was Professor of Biblical Studies at Columbia University.

THE REV. HUGH LISTER was an Anglican priest attached to Eton College Comm. in Hackney Wick in the East End of London. An early "worker priest," he worked with the unemployed and also with the trade unions. He enlisted in the British Army at the beginning of the war and was killed in France. Tillich was very impressed by him and with others who combined social passion with liturgical discipline.

JOHN H. OLDHAM was one of the most remarkable Protestant churchmen of the post-World War I period. An ordained English Congregational clergyman, he was one of the key architects of the planning for, and execution of, the Oxford Conference. He was profoundly interested in the involvement of the church in all aspects of cultural and social life.

Page 35

LORD LOTHIAN is the former Philip Ker. Lothian had been Ambassador to the United States. He was associated with the so-called Clivedon set and their policy.

Page 36

ARNOLD BÖCKLIN was a late nineteenth-century German painter who did a number of lovely landscapes.

Page 39

THE REV. R. H. EDWIN ESPY was at that time Secretary of the World Student Christian Federation. He is currently General Secretary of the National Council of the Churches of Christ in the U.S.A.

Page 40

THE RT. HON. ANTHONY WEDGEWOOD BENN, M.P., had been the British Secretary of State for India in the 1920's. Later, during the war, he was British Minister for Air. After the war he became Lord Stansgate.

Page 41

DR. BRUNO ADLER was connected with the Bauhaus group of architects and wrote under the name of Urban Roedl.

THE KUESSEL refers to a home owned jointly by Fritz and Lilly Pincus and Guenther and Claire Lowenfeld. It was joined by a bridge, and was located on an island just outside of Potsdam. Tillich wrote a special article on the occasion of the dedication of the Kuessel. He was a frequent visitor there, as the Lowenfelds and Pincuses were among his closest friends. The house was the center for much discussion among German intellectual friends of Tillich. Both families are referred to a number of times in the diary.

KARL MANNHEIM was a former Frankfurt colleague of Tillich who emigrated to England and later went to the United States. He was a very distinguished sociologist.

ADOLPH LOEWE was one of Tillich's closest personal friends and a very intimate co-worker in the religious socialist movement. An eminent economist, he fled Frankfurt, first settling in Manchester, England, and later moving to the New School for Social Research in New York. There are many references to him throughout the diary, usually as Adolph.

ELISABETH AND ERHARDT SEEBERGER are the younger sister and brother-in-law of Paul Tillich. Erhardt, a Lutheran pastor in Berlin, was active in the confessing church movement that opposed Hitler on neo-orthodox theological grounds. Tillich had his first reunion with them in Switzerland when they vacationed together beginning July 3. It is clear that he was eagerly looking forward to meeting them. Their names occur frequently in the diary. The Seebergers had three children, Hans Jürgen, Heide, and Waldtraud.

Page 42

A number of places in the diary TILLICH refers to his idea of a "religious order"

or to an "order." Discussion with Professors Loewe and Pauck lead one to think that Tillich had in mind the founding of a special international group of men profoundly concerned with thought and action in face of the world situation. These men would be leading intellectuals and men of affairs who together would meet regularly to analyze the key issues confronting mankind. Such mutual stimulation would lead to creative action on the part of men of affairs and to a more existential perspective on the part of intellectuals. Tillich thought of these men as comprising an order dedicated to certain common goals. Perhaps this idea influenced Oldham who later founded a somewhat similar group in England called the "Moot." Later he continued the concept in another English circle called the "Frontier" movement.
The reference to SIR WALTER MOBERLY as a "Ford" among the English aristocracy alludes to his rank as knight as being on the lowest order in the hierarchy of the aristocracy. In the 1930's the Ford was the lowest priced of American automobiles.

Page 43

The editor of the *Economist* referred to was Geoffry Crowther.

Page 44

ARNOLD NASH was a young English clergyman who worked very closely with Sir Walter Moberly and was deeply interested in social problems, especially the nature of higher education. For a number of years he has been a professor at the University of North Carolina.

Page 45

TEDDY refers to Professor Theodore Adorno, a distinguished sociologist and philosopher who was a colleague and friend of Tillich at Frankfurt. He emigrated to England where he taught at Merton College, Oxford. Later he taught in the United States, returning after the war to Frankfurt.

Page 47

GERHARD MEYER met Tillich at Frankfurt and was very active in the youth movement of religious socialism. He later went to the United States where he became a professor at the University of Chicago.

Page 48

JOHN AND MARY STOCKS were both philosophers from Oxford, teaching at Manchester University. After John Stocks' death, Dr. Mary Stocks had a distinguished career as Head of Westfield College of London University.

Page 49

PROFESSOR JOHN BAILLIE was one of Scotland's most distinguished and productive theological scholars in the twentieth century. He became principal of the theological college at the University of Edinburgh. He knew Tillich from Union Theological Seminary.

Page 51

PROFESSOR H. R. MACKINTOSH was professor of systematic theology at New College, Edinburgh University.

Page 52

IAN BAILLIE is the son of John Baillie.
NORMAN KEMP-SMITH was a distinguished Professor of Philosophy at Edinburgh.

Page 53

PROFESSOR FREDERICK POLLOCK was a friend of Tillich from Frankfurt. He was a collaborator with Professor Horkheimer in the Institute for Social Research at Frankfurt.

REINHOLD SCHAIRER was a founder of an international student service organization and was thoroughly familiar with youth problems in Germany.

Page 55

WALDEMAR SCHACHT was Finance Minister in the Third Reich.

ELSA BRANSTROM was known as the angel of Siberia. She went to Siberia after World War I to aid the starving children and won acclaim for her humanity.

DR. OTTO CAHN-FREUD was a distinguished jurist who was one of the first to leave Nazi Germany. He became a lecturer at the London School of Economics.

HUGO SINSHEIMER was a jurist who emigrated to Holland.

THE REV. CANON BARRY, F. R., was Theologian and then Canon Residentuary of Westminster Abbey. After, he became Bishop of Southwell.

Page 56

KERRL was Interior Minister in Nazi Germany in 1936. He was one of the key figures in the Nazi government responsible for determining which German should be free to attend the Oxford Conference.

Page 57

PROFESSOR ERNST KANTOROWITZ had been a professor of history at the University of Frankfurt and a friend of Tillich.

Page 58

HAROLD POELCHAU was a student of Tillich. He became active in social welfare work, and was a member of the religious socialist group.

AUGUST RATHMANN was a member of the Democratic Socialist Party, a friend of Poelchau and Tillich, and a member of the religious socialist circle.

THEODORE HAUBACH was a member of the Democratic Socialist Party and part of the resistance group of July 20, 1944. He was executed by the Nazis in January, 1945.

PROFESSOR EMIL FUCHS had been a founder of the religious socialist movement and professor of systematic theology at the Pedagogical Institute of Kiel. He was forcibly retired by the Nazis. His son was Klaus Fuchs, convicted of turning over atomic secrets to the Russians.

CHRISTIAN HERMANN was a teacher in a Gymnasium and an old close friend of Tillich.

Page 61

HERMANN OLDEN wrote one of the very first books on Hitler; it appeared in 1933.

HEIDEN wrote a book very critical of Hitler; it was banned from Germany.

DR. JOHN MAUD, a Christian layman who was very active in the preparation for the Oxford Conference. Then Dean of University College, Oxford. Later Permanent Under-Secretary in Ministry of Education, then High Commissioner in South Africa. He is now Lord Redcliff-Maud, Master of University College, Oxford.

Page 62

MRS. MELLINGER was a Jungian psychoanalyist who came from Berlin.

FREDERICH SPIEGELBERG was a professor of history of religions, a specialist in Hinduism. He was a younger friend of Tillich.

JUNG'S Eranos circle was a yearly seminar that met at the estate of Frau Froebe-Kuptein in Ascona, Switzerland. It grew out of discussions between Rudolf Otto and Frau Froebe, and C. G. Jung, famous psychiatrist, became the intellectual godfather for the meetings. The great intellectuals from a number of nations gathered to read papers subsequently published in a yearbook. There was always a central theme for each annual meeting.

Page 63

DEMUTH was a former secretary of the Berlin Chamber of Commerce. He ran a special refugee program for placing academic emigrees in England.

Page 64

KAROLUS MENNICKE was one of Tillich's closest friends. He was a theologian and a founder of the Berlin circle of the "Papers on Religious Socialism" on which he worked with Tillich.

Page 67

DR. AND MRS. IDE were leading Dutch citizens; Mrs. Ide was a patroness for Karolus Mennicke.

Page 72

STEPHAN HIRZEL was the architect who designed the Küssel in Potsdam.

Page 73

REVESZ was a psychologist from Hungary who was a friend of Dr. Kurt Goldstein in Frankfurt.

Page 77

MOISSI was one of the most famous actors in Germany at that time.

Page 79

M. L. refers to Hannah's sister M. L. Werner, the psychoanalyist from Berlin.

Page 83

WILHELM STAEHLIN was a theologian and minister who developed a concept of a Protestant religious order and led a movement to revitalize liturgical life in the Lutheran and Evangelical churches.

GERMAN CHRISTIANS were those churchmen, clergy and laymen, who agreed with Nazi efforts to purge the churches of all Jewish influence and who understood the churches to be a special facet of the total German people.

Page 84

BERNEUCHNER BROTHERHOOD was created and led by Staehlin as the first step in his effort to recreate Protestant liturgical life. It was a Protestant brotherhood, but it was in the world bound together by common discipline, liturgical life, and theological analysis.

FREDE was Tillich's brother-in-law of whom he was very fond. Frede's wife Johanna, Tillich's sister, had died and Frede later married Trudschen.

KARL RITTER was a theologian and colleague of Staehlin who helped to lead the Berneuchner circle in which Tillich was deeply interested.

Page 86

PAUL OPPENHEIM and his wife Gaby were from Frankfurt where he was a leading businessman and an independent philosopher. He later went from Belgium to England to the United States. They were very close friends of Tillich.

Page 90

PROFESSOR MARTIN HEIDEGGER of Marburg University is one of the great philosophical minds of the twentieth century.

PROFESSOR CARL G. HEMPEL is a noted philosopher and Berlin member of the "Vienna Circle." He later emigrated to the United States.

PROFESSOR RUDOLF CARNAP, original member of the "Vienna Circle," became Professor of Philosophy at Prague in 1933, then went to the University of Chicago.

DE MAN was a Belgian socialist who went to Frankfurt, held a teaching post, and joined the religious socialist circle. In 1933 he returned to Belgium and became a neo-Fascist, later holding the office of Prime Minister of Belgium. After the war he went to Switzerland.

PROFESSOR KURT RIEZLER, an eminent philosopher, had also been curator at the University of Frankfurt.

PROFESSOR WERNER JAEGER, the great classical scholar, first taught for many years at the University of Chicago and then went to Harvard University.

ECKHART VON SYDOW was one of Tillich's most intimate friends who first helped him to understand modern art and to develop a genuine competence in art criticism. He was a gifted historian of art.

PROFESSOR KARL REINHARDT was a former colleague of Tillich at Frankfurt.

PAUL HAGEN (pseudonym for Dr. Karl Frank) was a devoted anti-Nazi active in the underground. Hagen was associated with the "New Beginnings" group. He was instrumental in creating The American Friends of German Freedom, and later the Emergency Rescue Committee, both in the United States. He died in 1969.

PROFESSOR FRITZ LIEB was a theologian and member of the religious socialist movemnt before he emigrated to Switzerland.

PROFESSOR K. L. SCHMIDT was visiting professor of New Testament at Basel.

PROFESSOR KARL BARTH of Basel was one of the theological giants and a theological opponent of Tillich.

PROFESSOR ERIC SEEBERG was a theologian at the University of Berlin and son of the famous historical theologian Reinhold Seeburg.

PROFESSOR FRITZ MEDICUS was Tillich's professor of philosophy at the University of Halle who emigrated to Switzerland and taught at the University of Zurich.

FRITZ LANGHOF was a very creative German Communist playwright and good friend of Brecht. (The "Moorsoldaten" became the song of the concentration camps.)

HENDRIK EISENSTEIN was one of the leading directors and producers of films in Russia during the twenties and thirties.

EMIL BRUNNER was one of the outstanding Swiss theologians of the thirties and forties. Though he disagreed with Barth, he disagreed also with Tillich.

ARNOLD AND DORIS WOLFERS were close friends of Tillich. He, Belgian born, had been head of Hochschule Politik in Berlin. Later Professor of International Relations and Master of Pierson College, and Dean of Graduate Studies in Social Sciences, Yale University. After leaving Yale, was Director of Institute for Foreign Policy Research in Washington, D.C. He died in 1967.

Page 140

EMIL AND SUZANNE BLUM were friends of Tillich from the religious socialist days in Germany. Blum was coeditor with Hermann Schaaft and Tillich of the periodical *Newwork*. He returned to his native Switzerland in 1933.

Page 141

WILHELM PAUCK, a friend and former student of Tillich, was then teaching at the University of Chicago.

PROFESSOR ADOLF KELLER was a famous Swiss theologian and ecumenical churchman.

BASSERMANN was a great German actor who fled Germany and took with him the Iffland ring, symbol of supremacy on the German stage.

Page 143

HEINRICH BRUENING was former Chancellor of Germany.

Page 145

FJEDOR STEPUN was a Russian refugee and former colleague of Tillich at Dresden. He was a mystic and a historian. Later he settled in Paris.

Page 148

DR. HANS LILJE was a Lutheran minister who was imprisoned by the Nazis because of his opposition to Hitler. He became a bishop and was an outstanding ecumenical churchman.

Page 149

PROFESSOR PAUL ALTHAUS was a Lutheran theologian at Erlangen.

Page 152

HEINRICH GOESCH held doctorates of law and philosophy. He was one of Tillich's closest friends and influenced him especially with respect to art and psychoanalysis. He was a brilliant conversationalist. Full reference to him begins on August 10.

Page 153

FIDES was the daughter of Heinrich Goesch.
KAETE was Goesch's widow.

Page 157

ADOLF REICHWEIN was a member of the resistance movement against the Nazis and later was executed by them.

Page 159

MARTIN BUBER was the eminent Jewish theologian and philosopher who also was a good friend of Tillich.
The conversation with FJEDOR STEPUN is about former colleagues at the University of Dresden.

Page 177

Peter refers to Eduard Heimann (see above reference to page 31).

192

70 71 72 73 10 9 8 7 6 5 4 3 2 1